Adult Coloring Book Mandalas Design
40 Relax Design

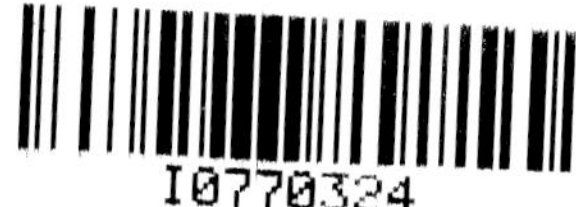

Adult Coloring Book Mandalas Design

ISBN-13: 978-1978246058

ISBN-10: 1978246056

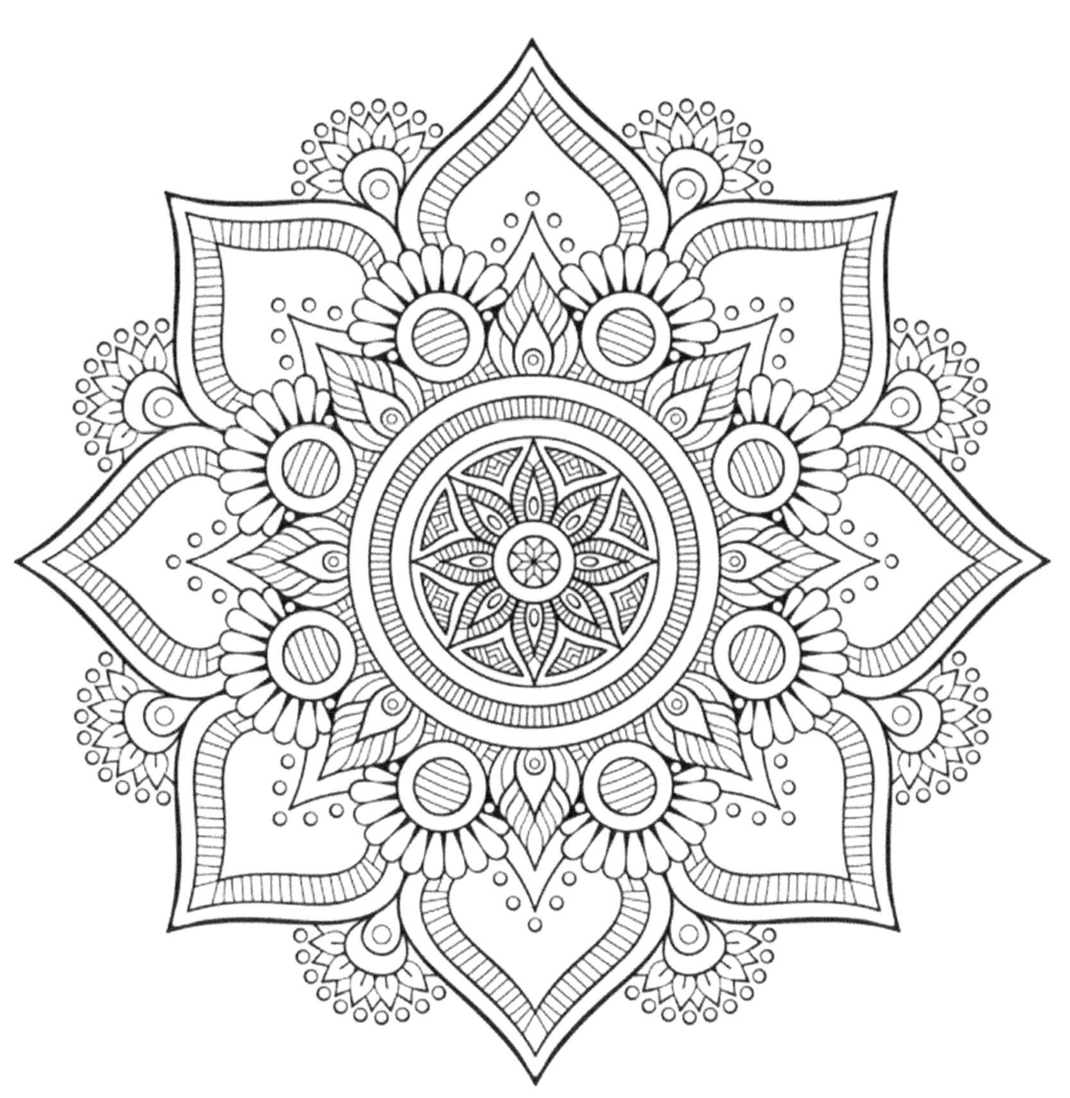

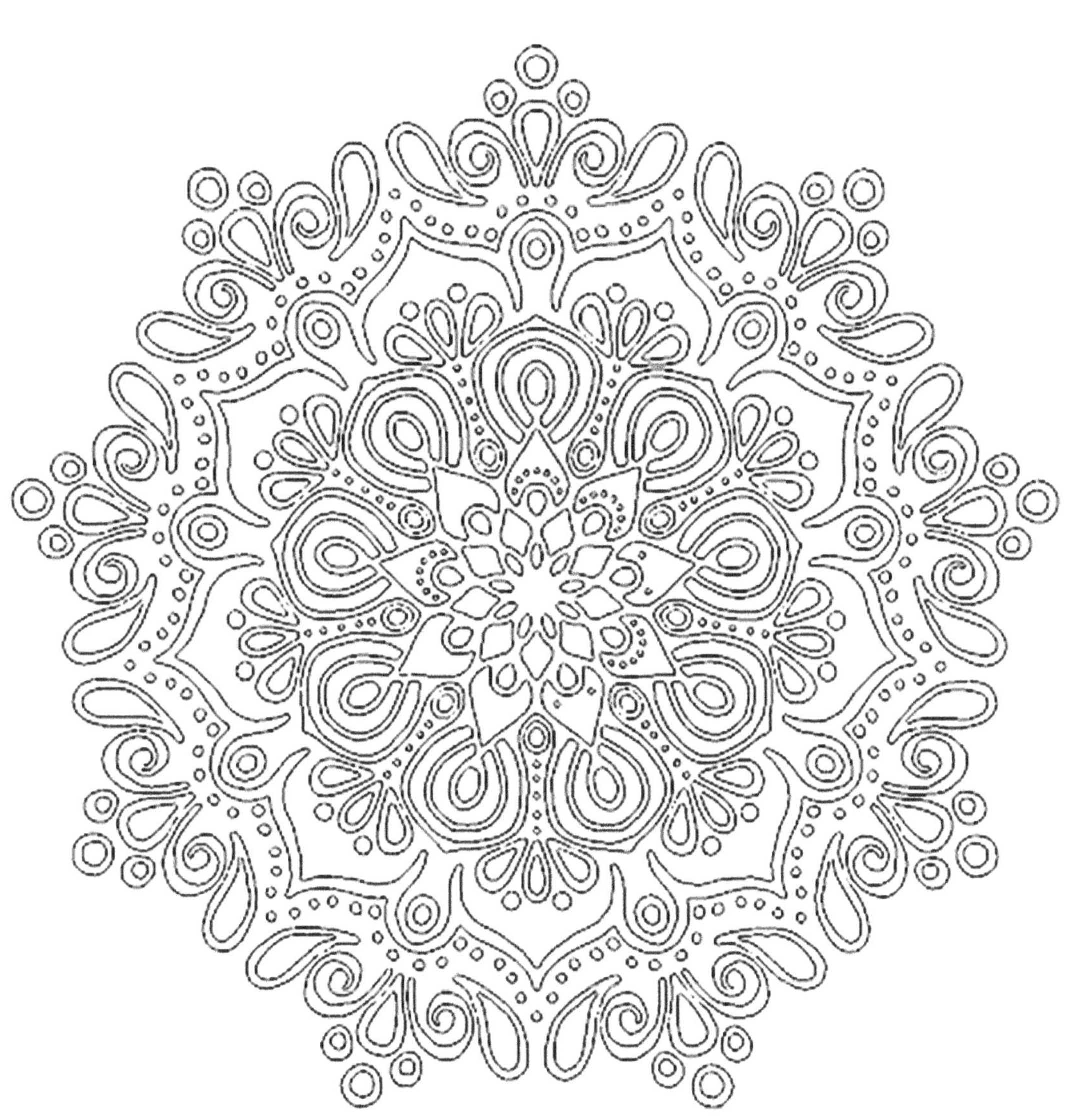

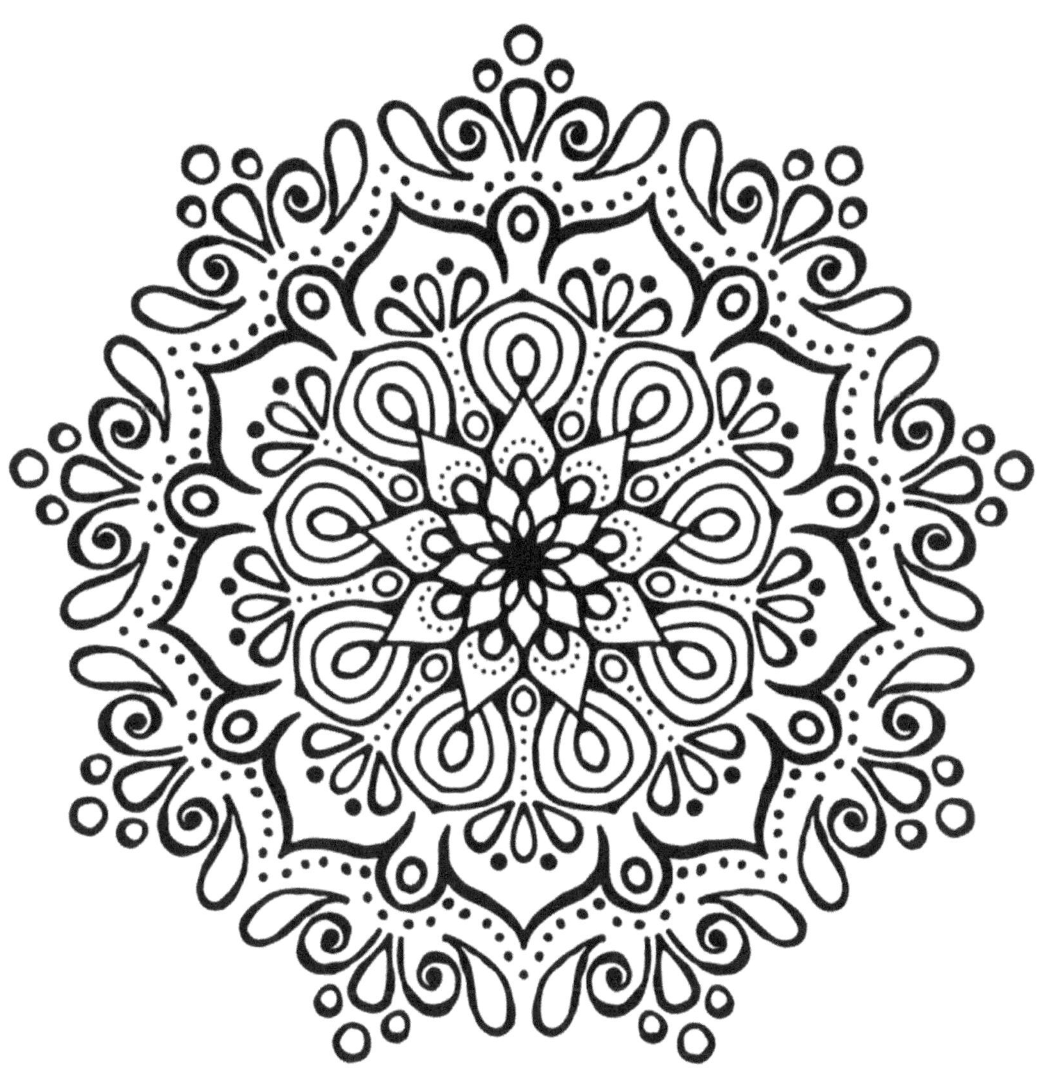

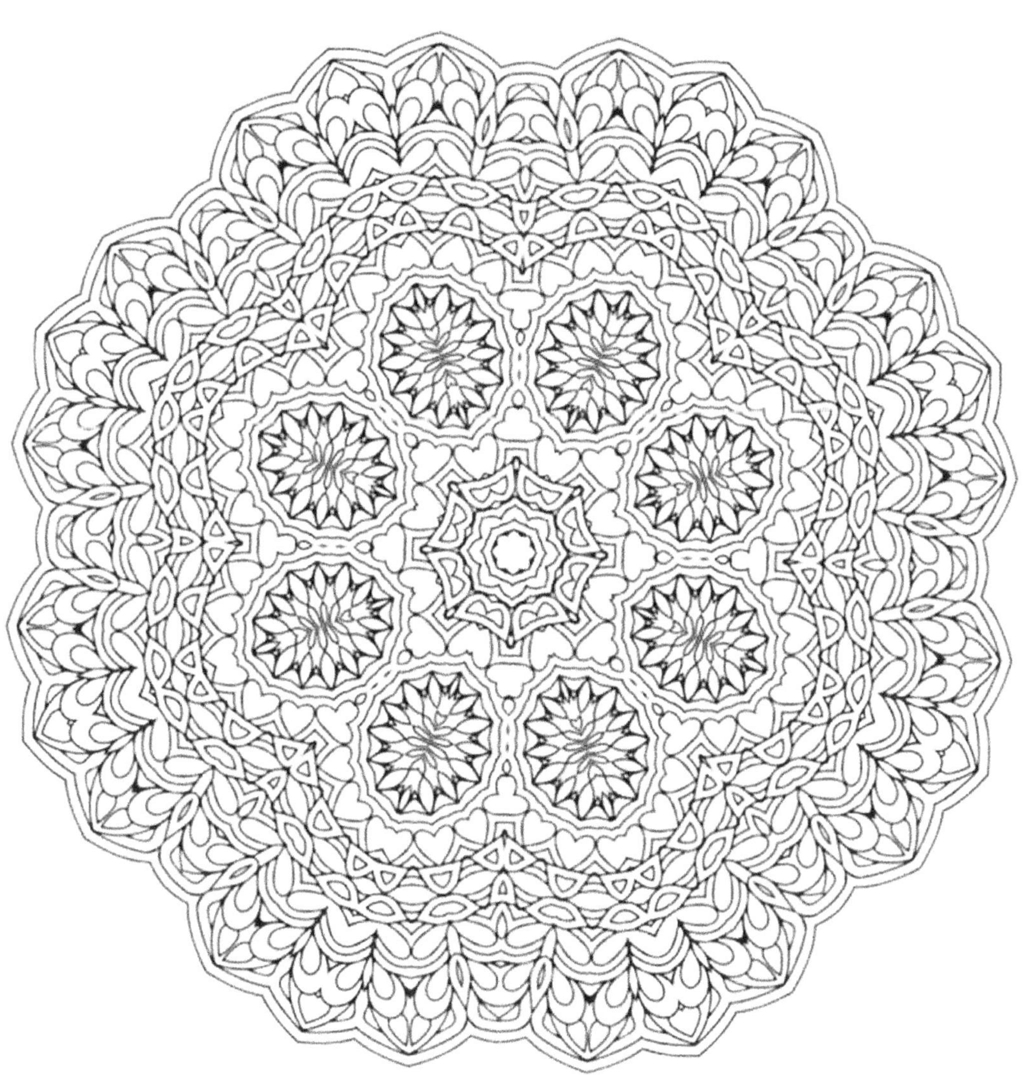

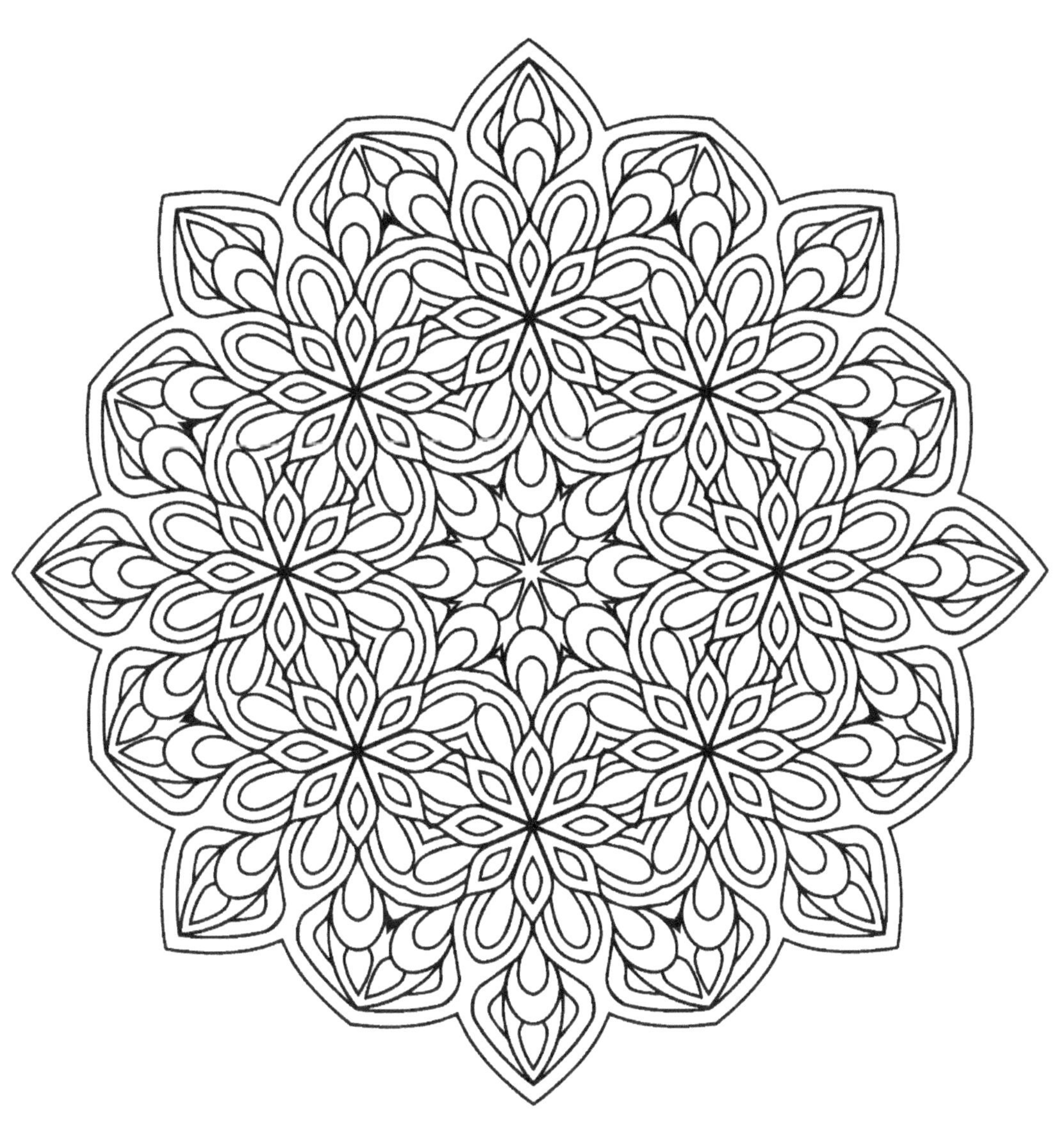

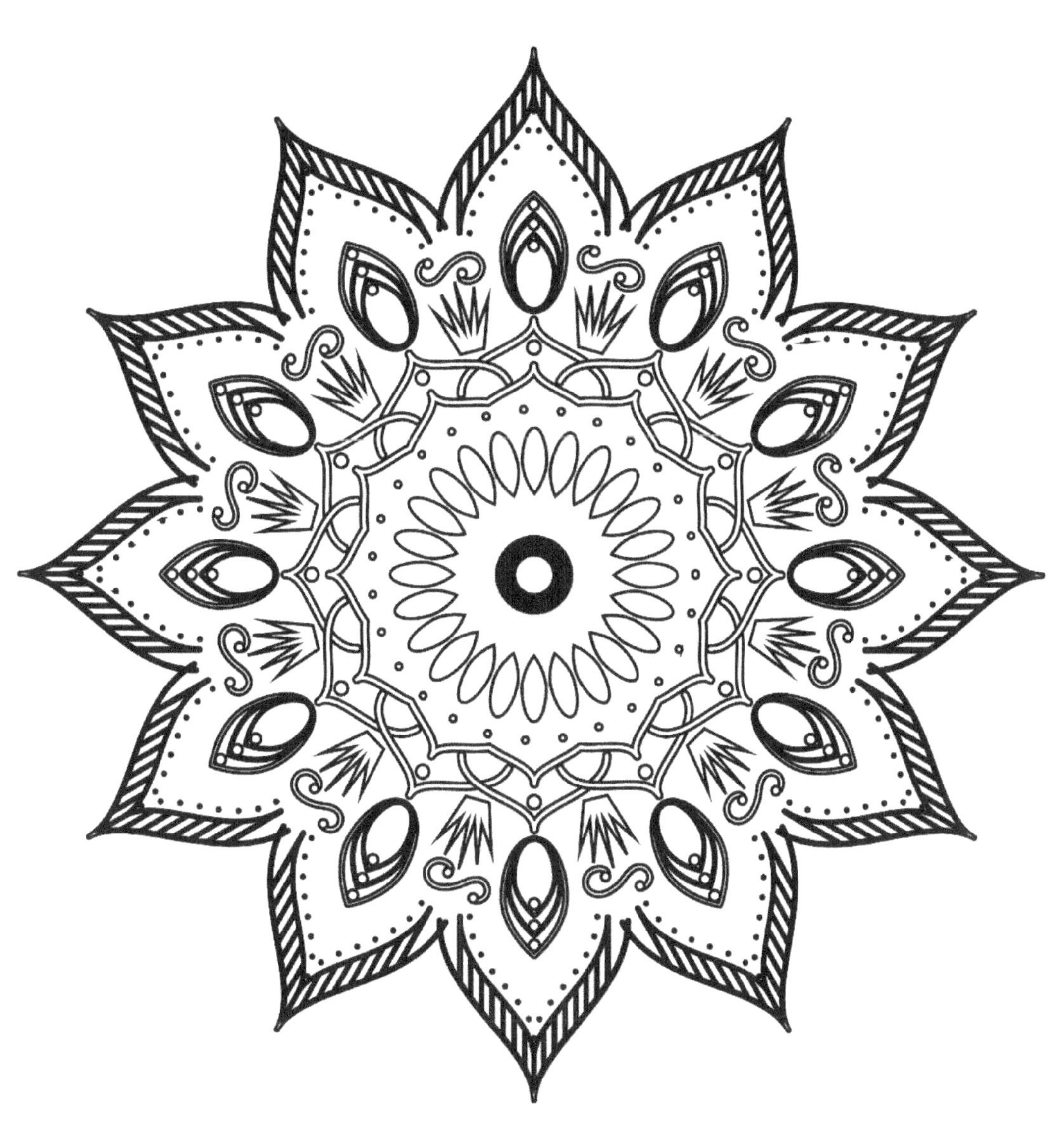

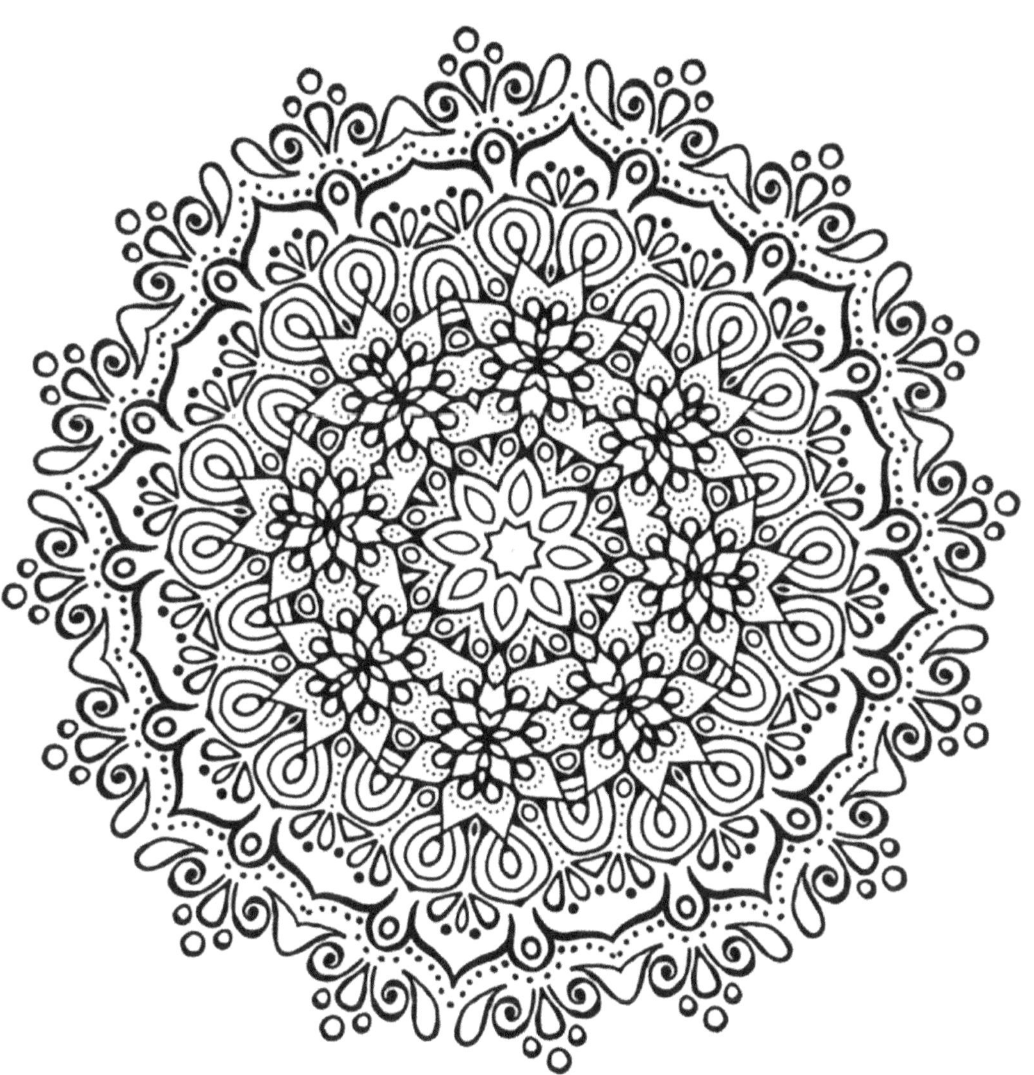

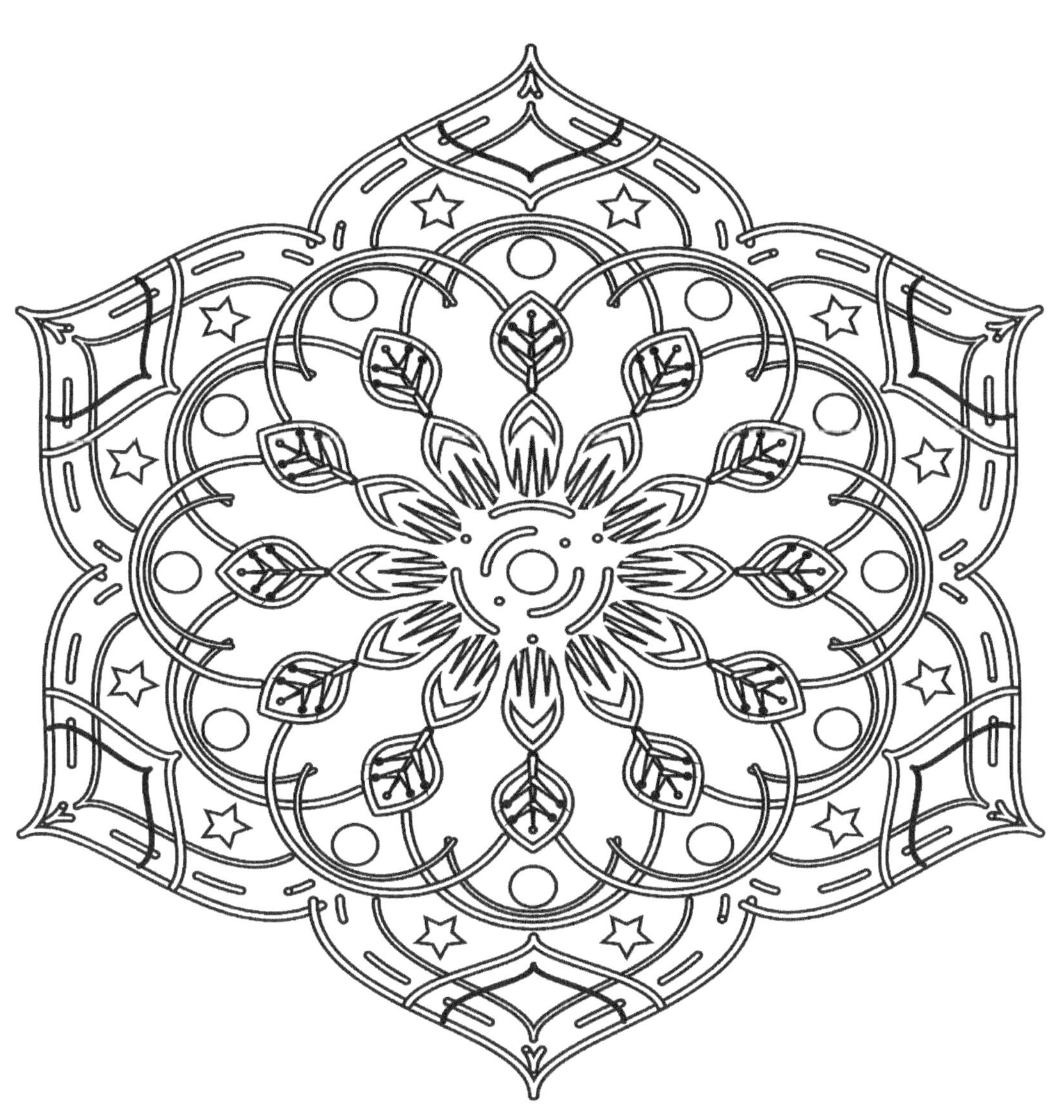

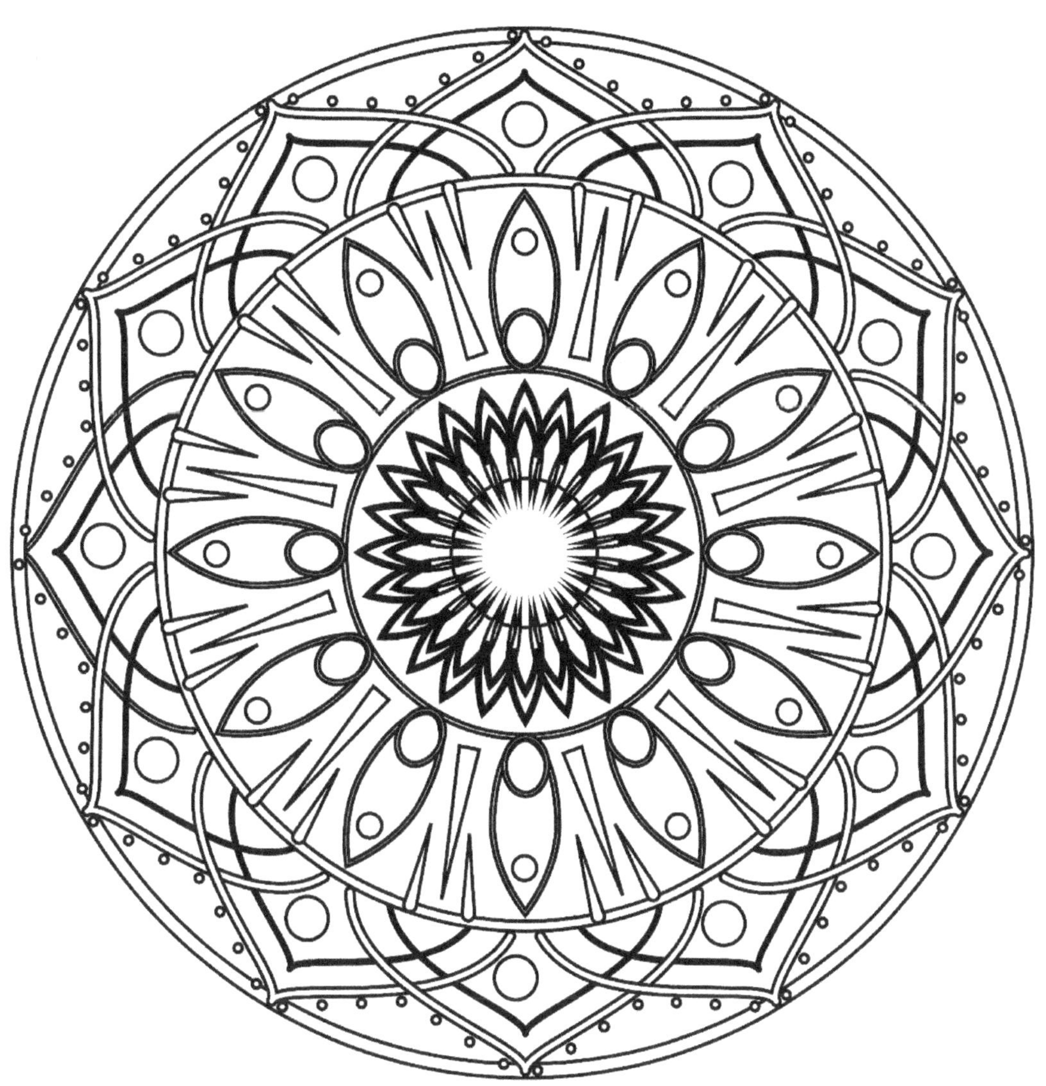

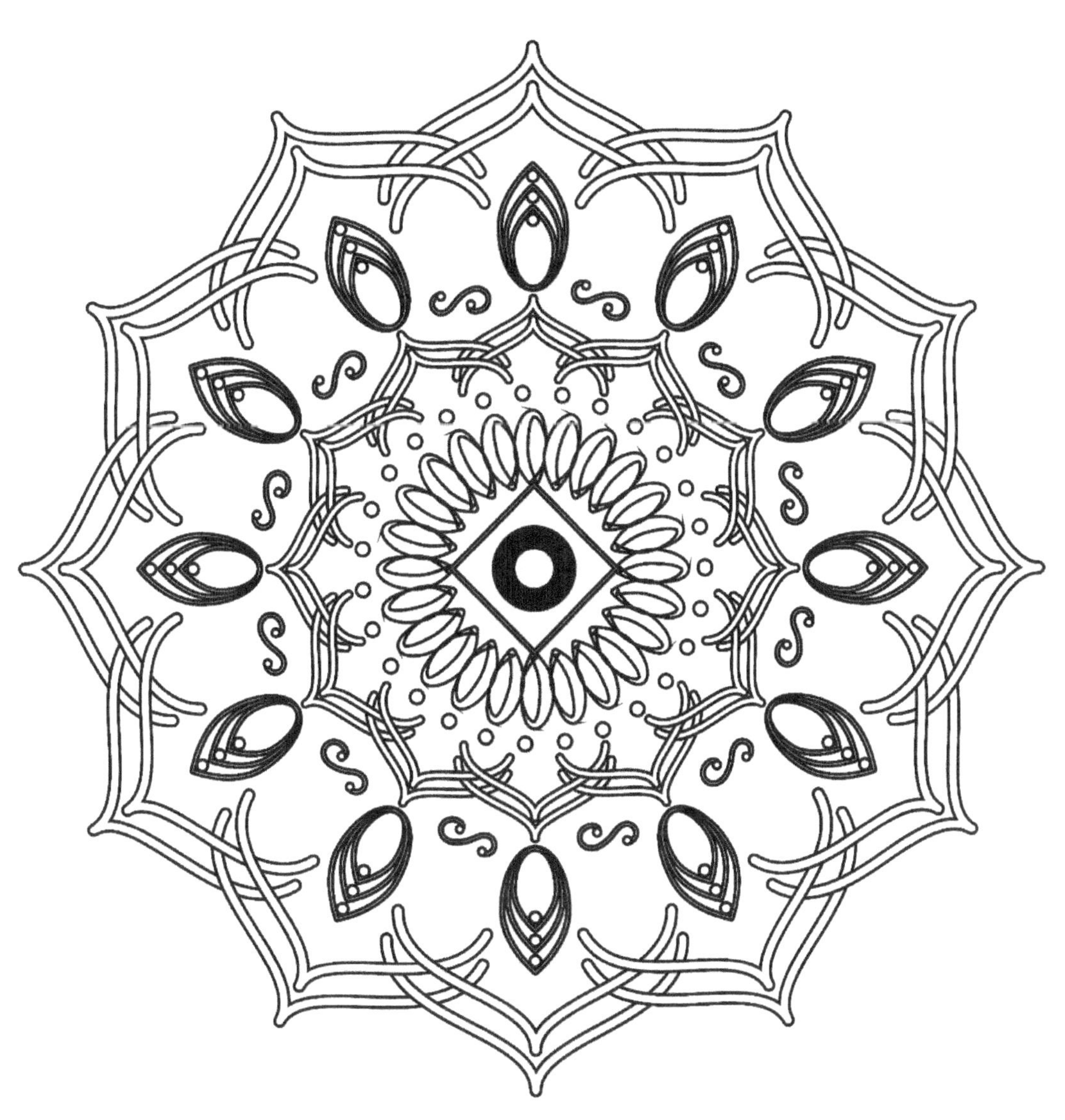

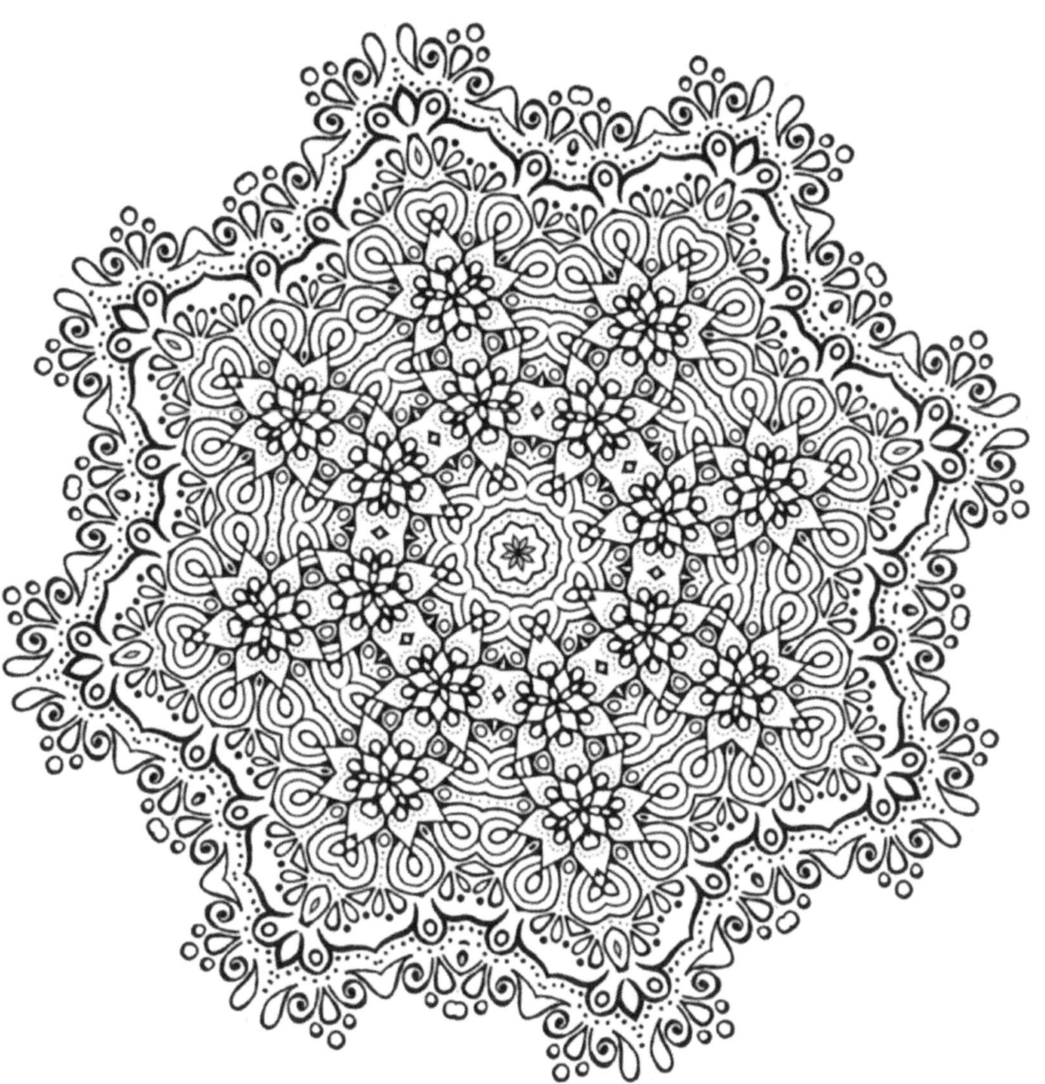

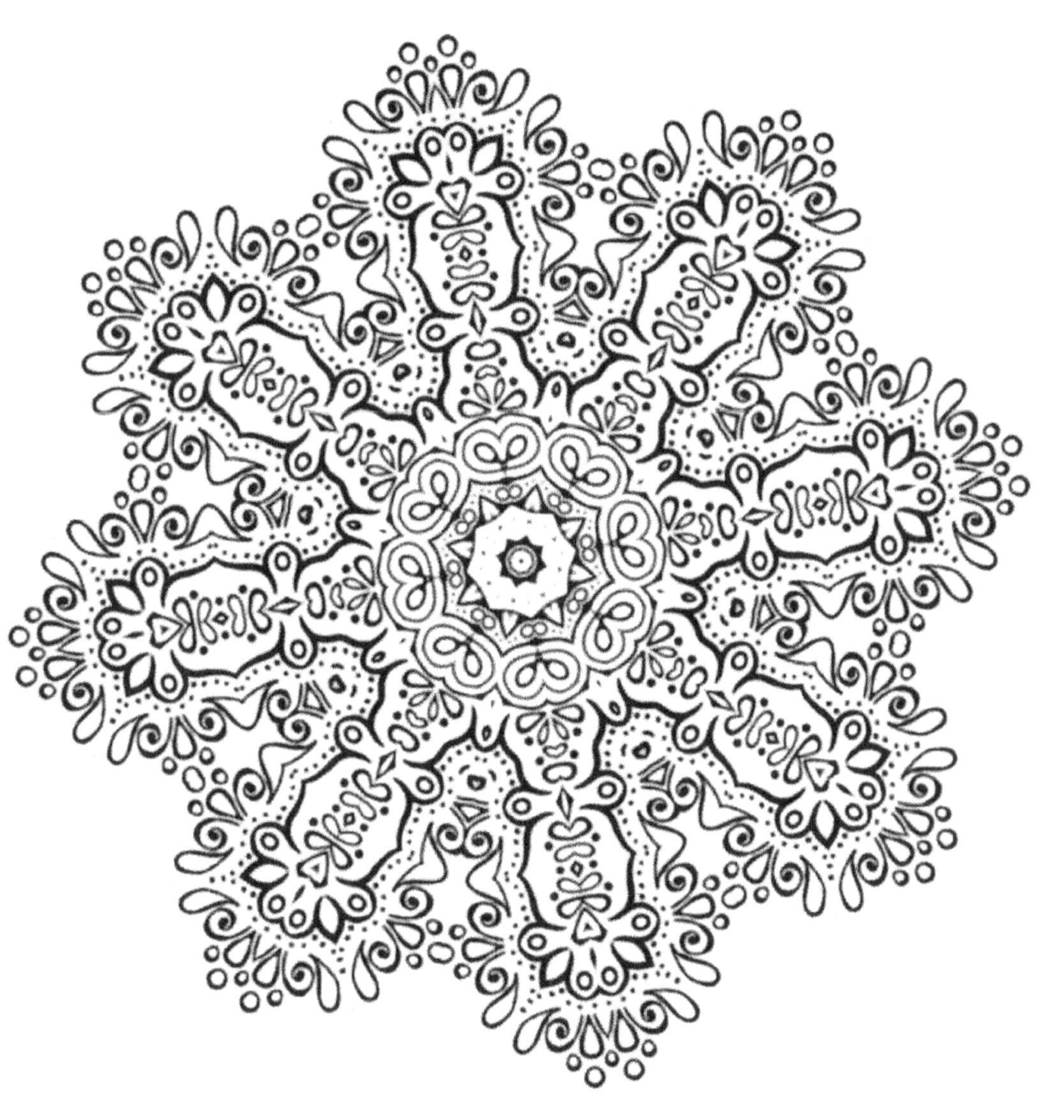

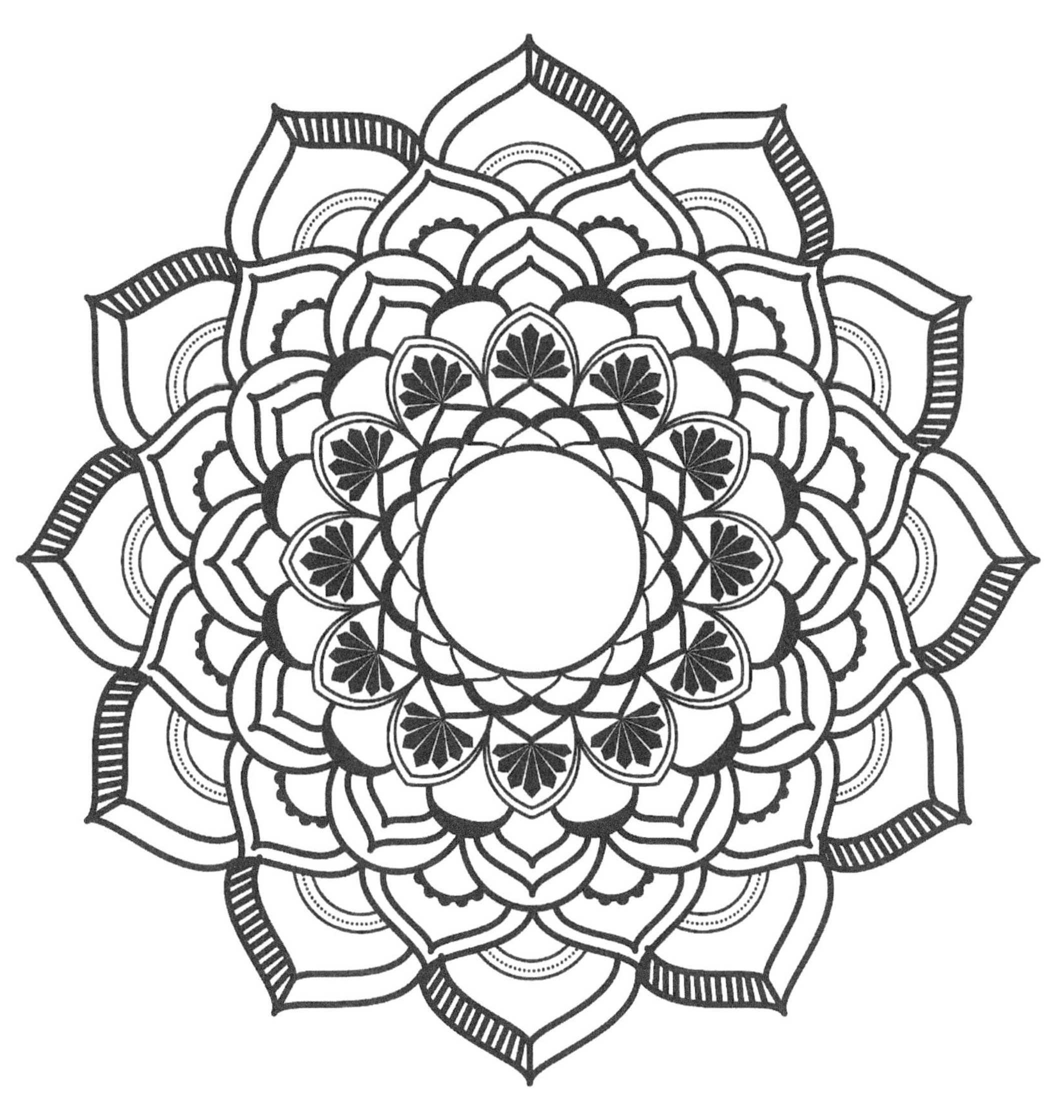

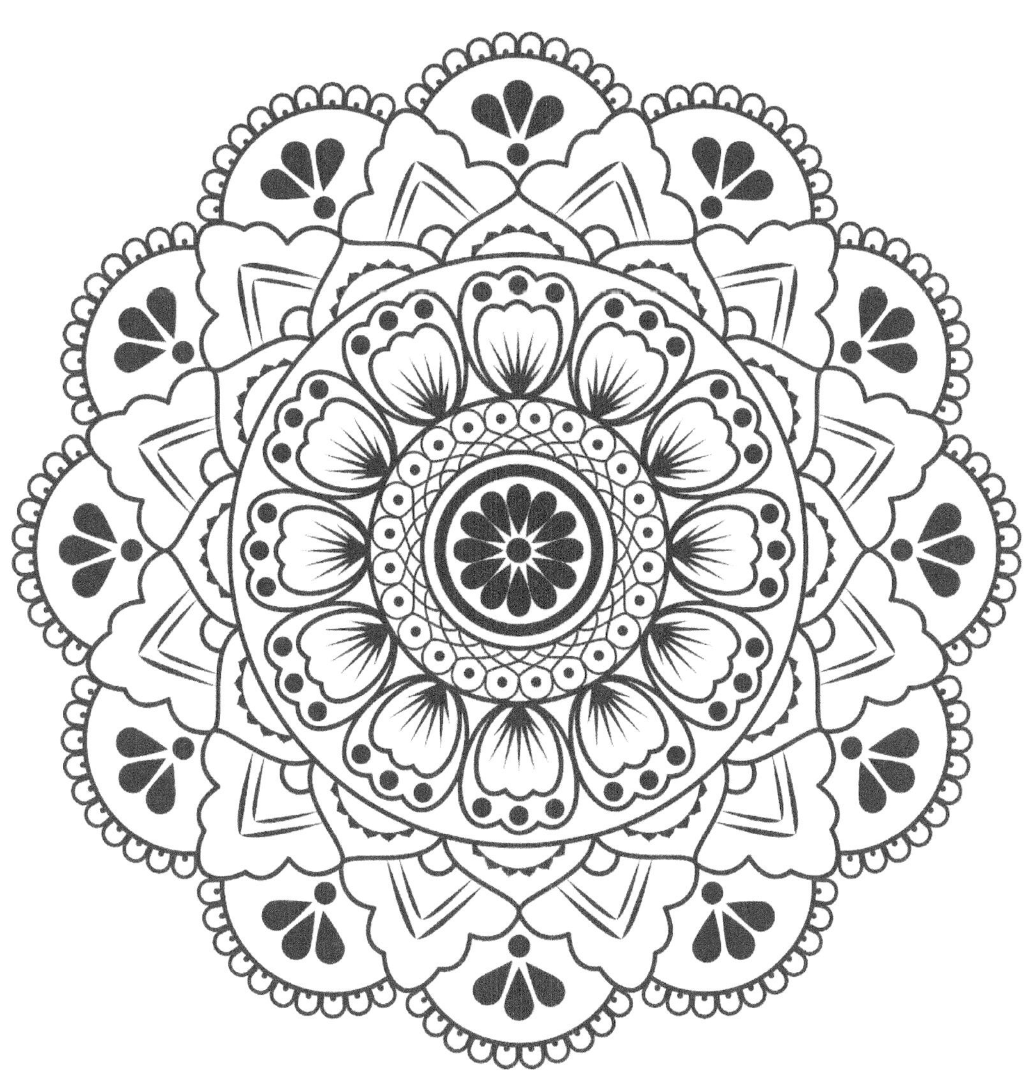

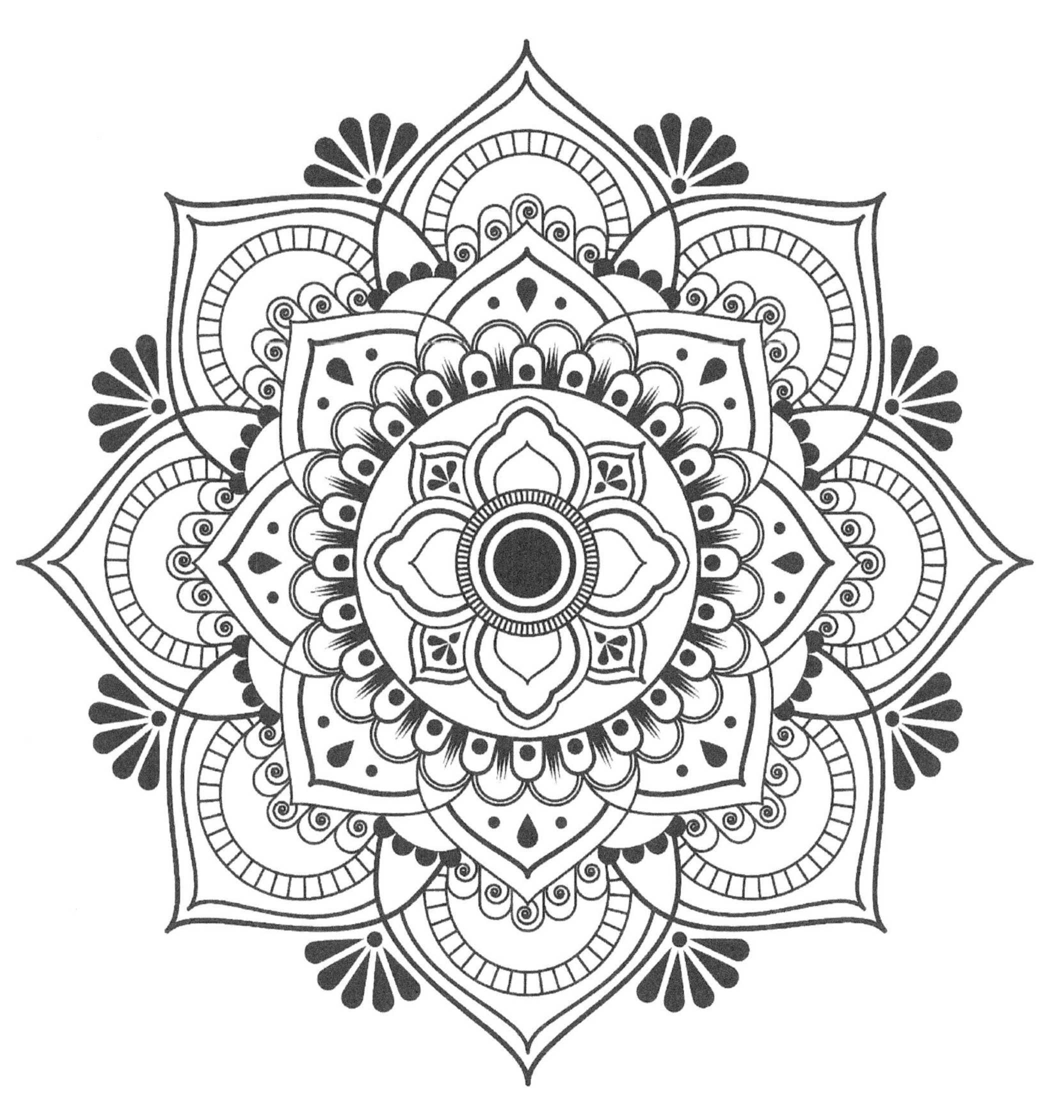

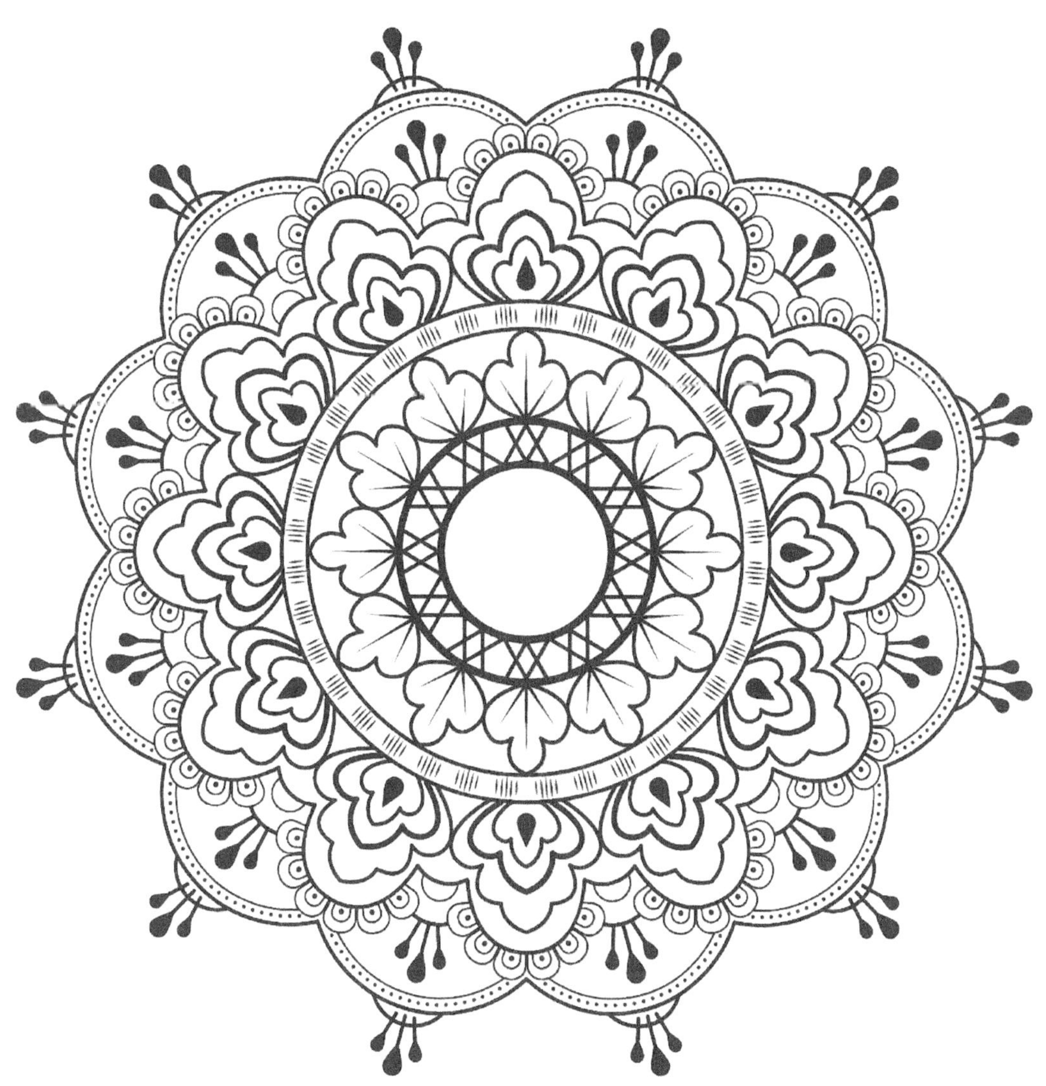

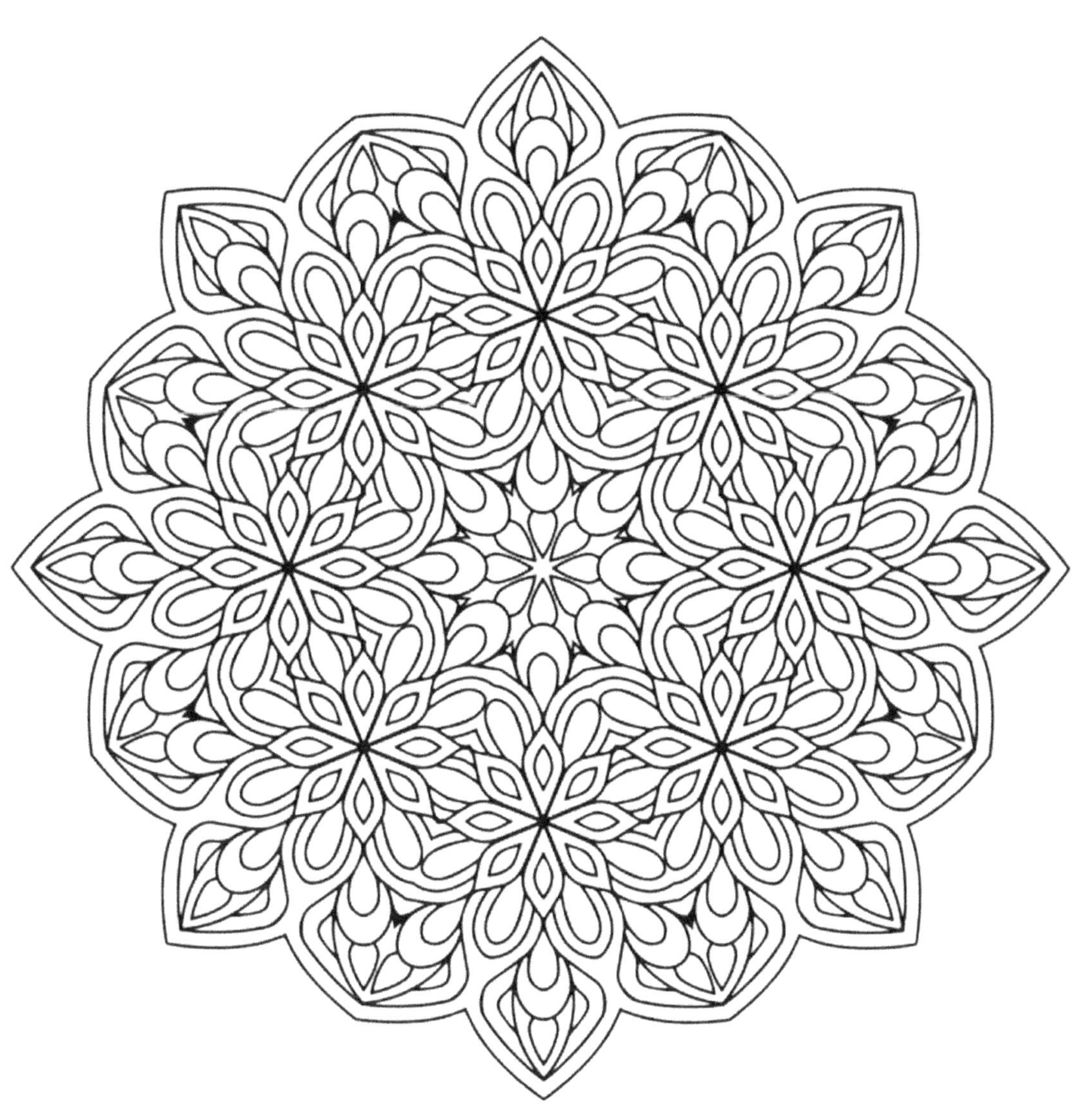

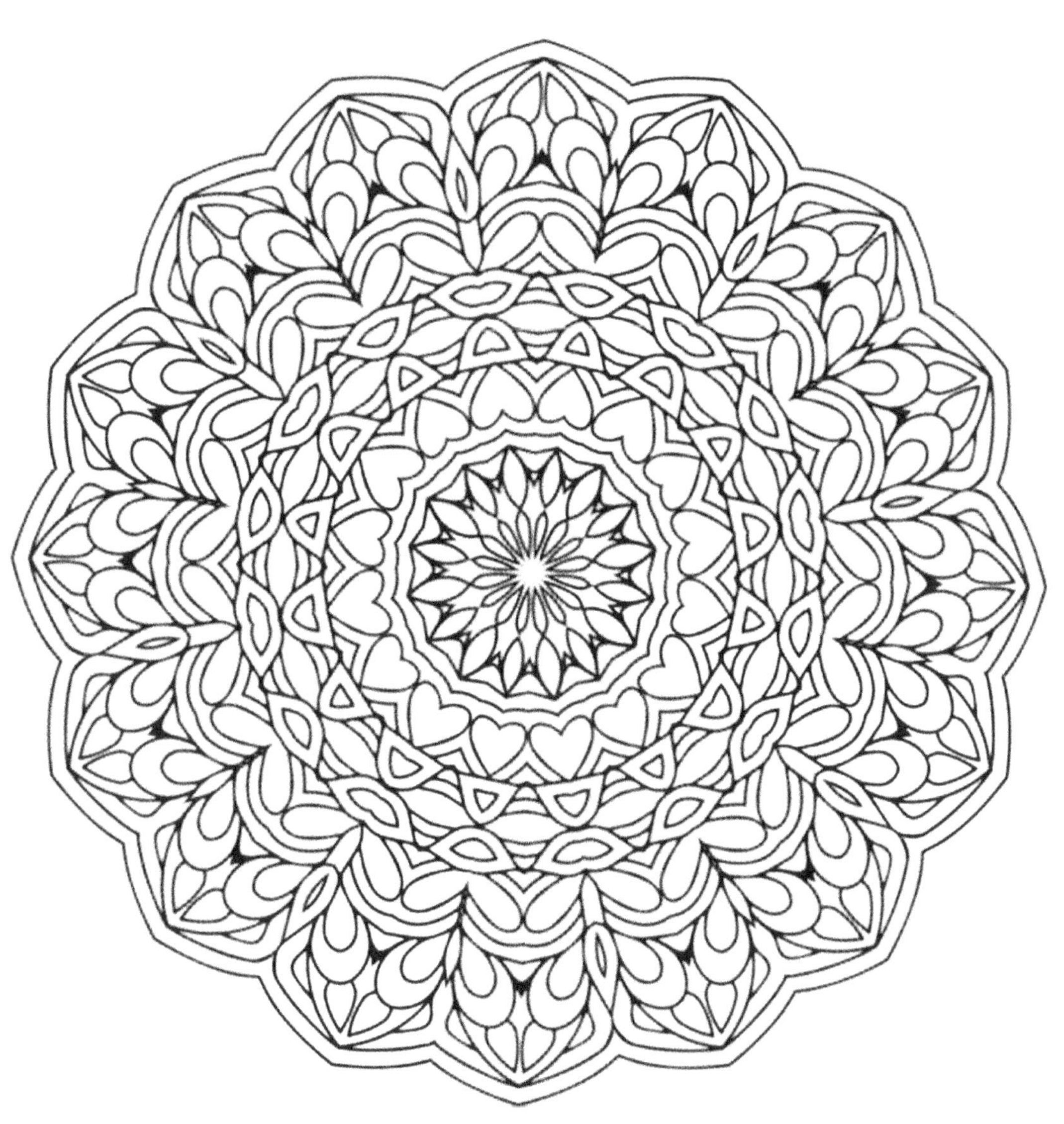

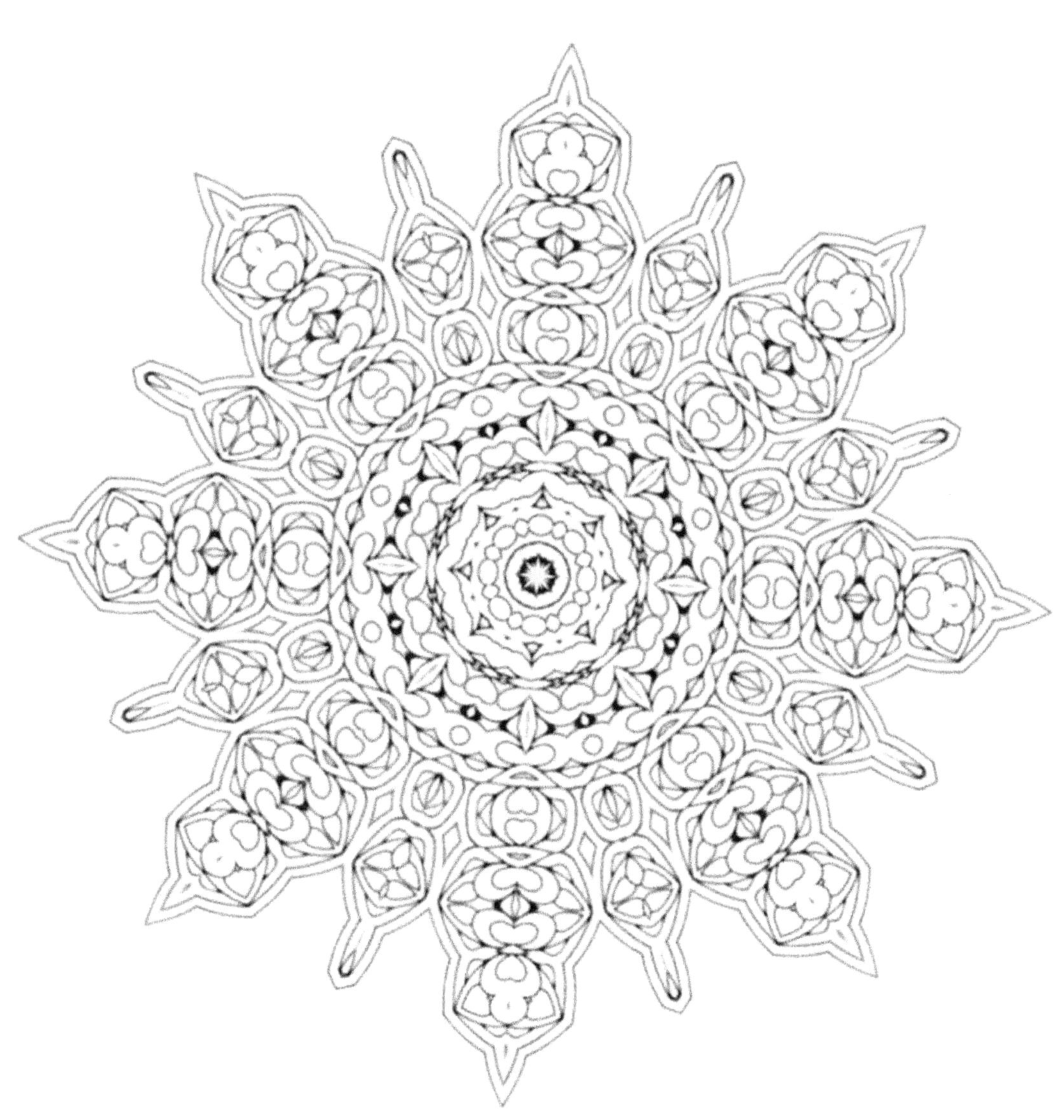

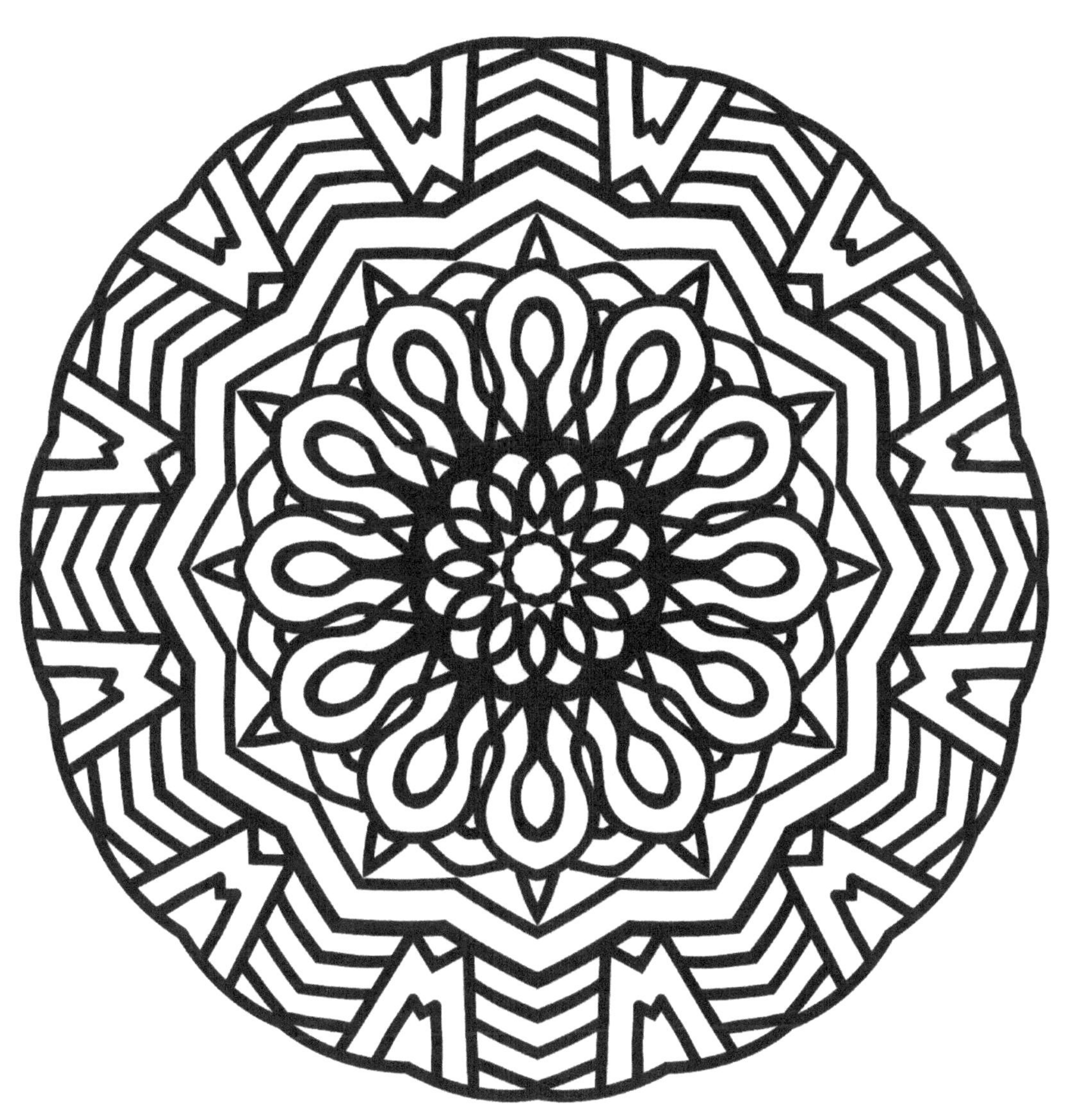

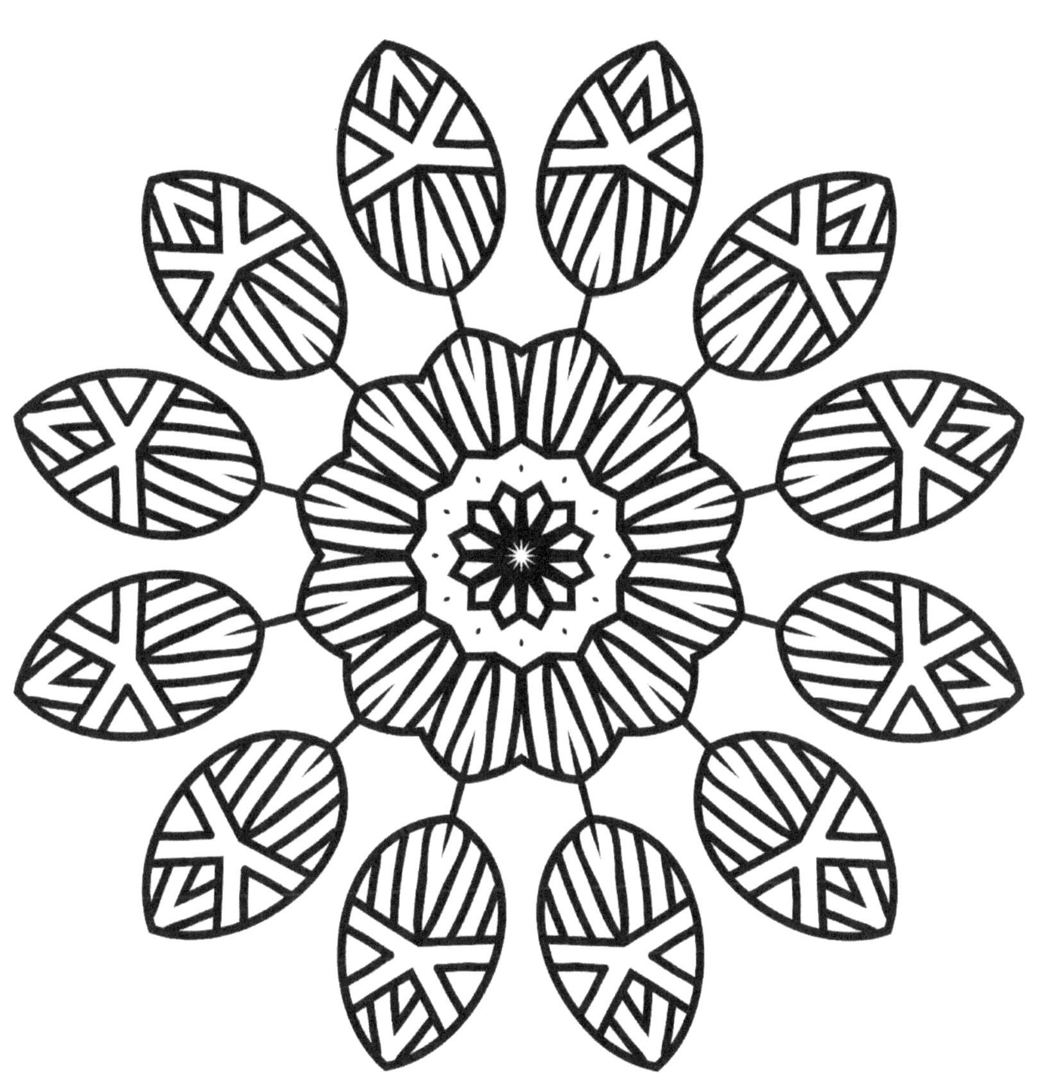

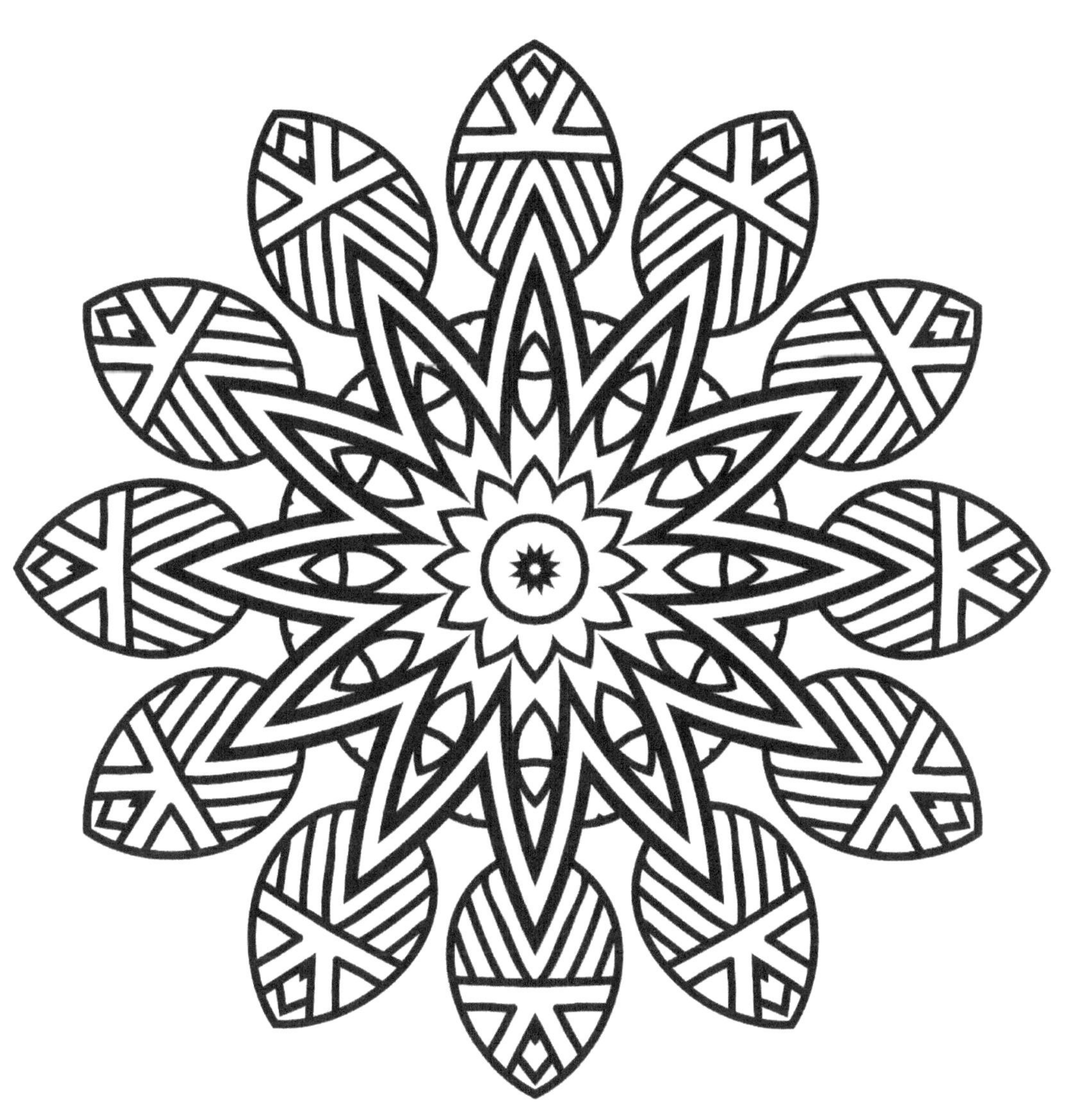

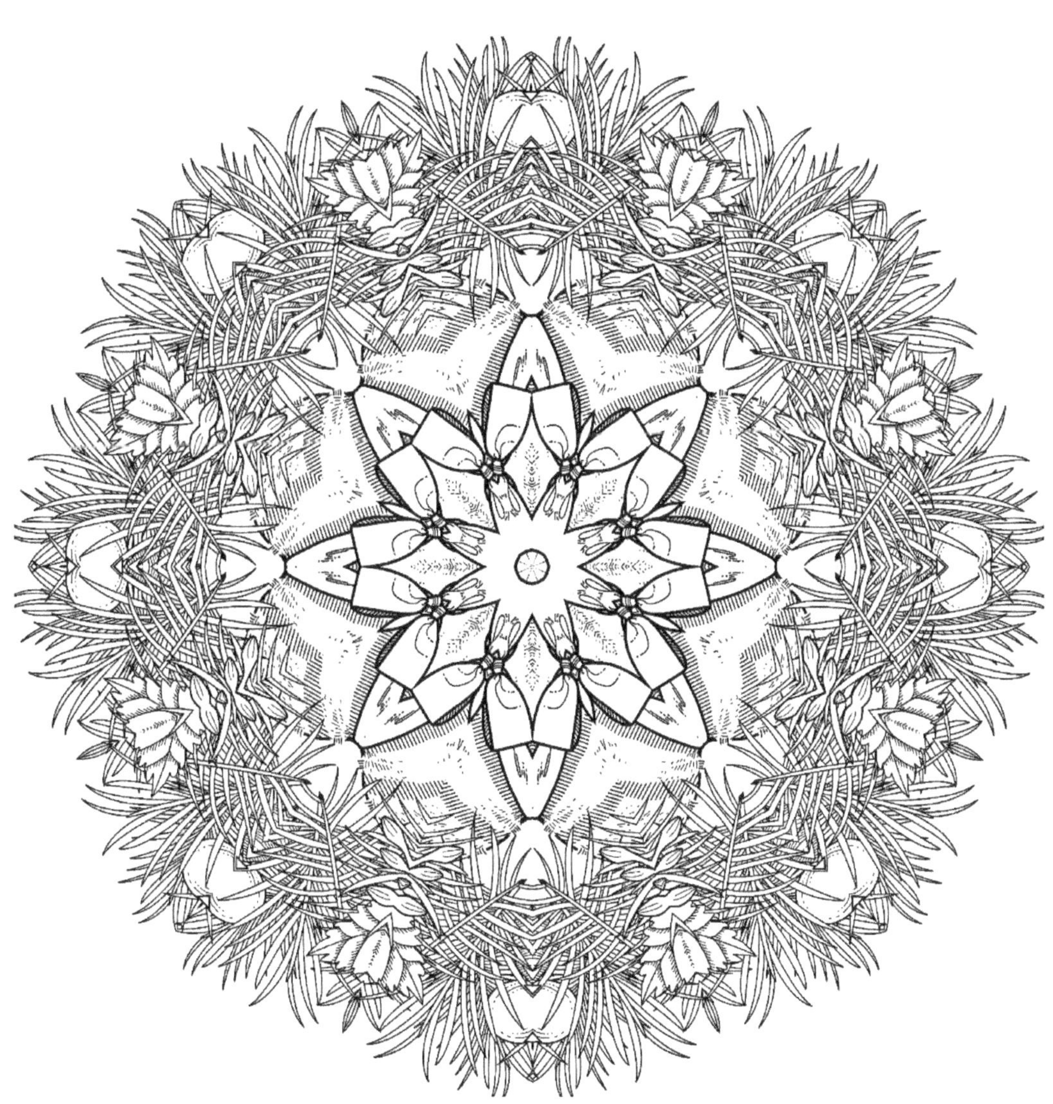

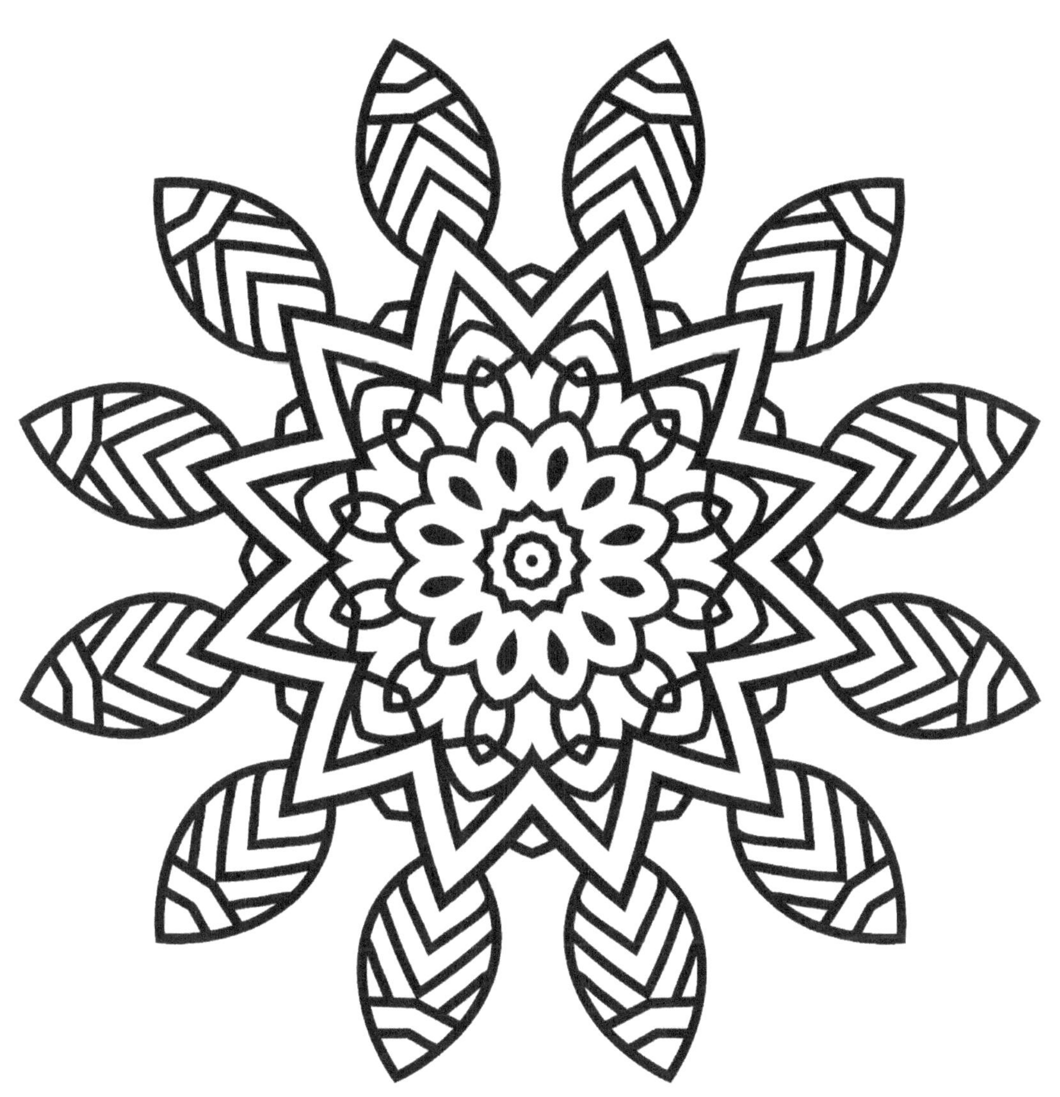

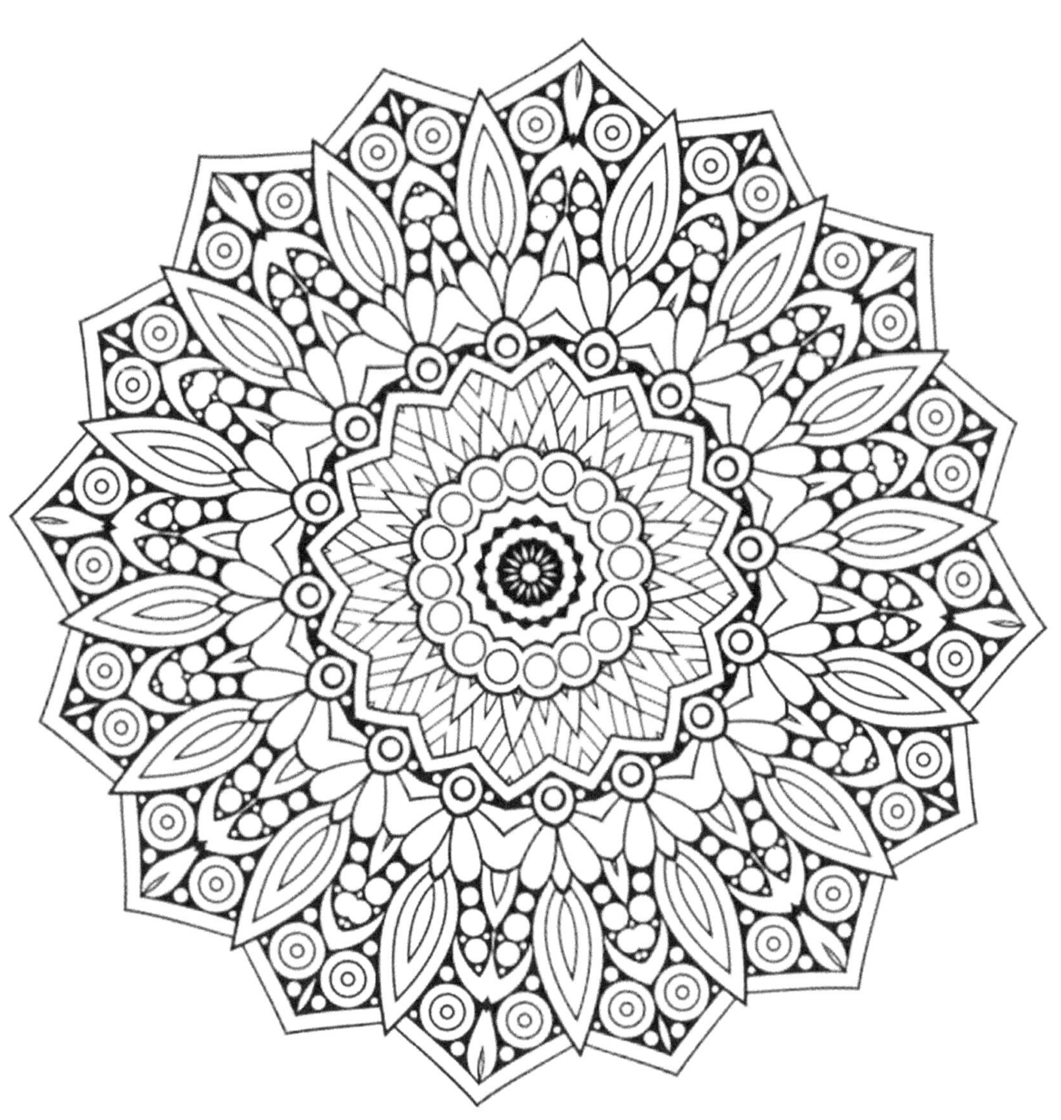

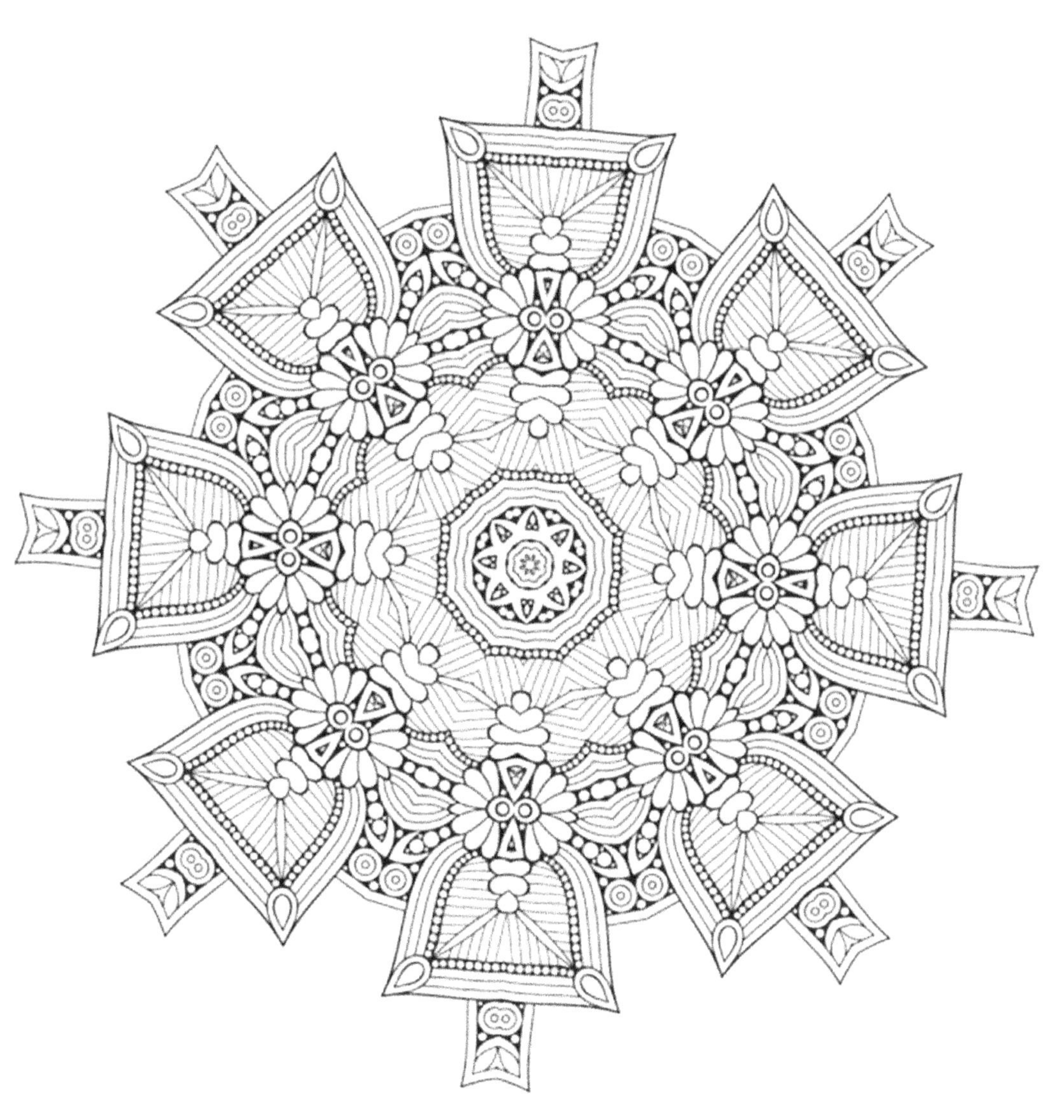

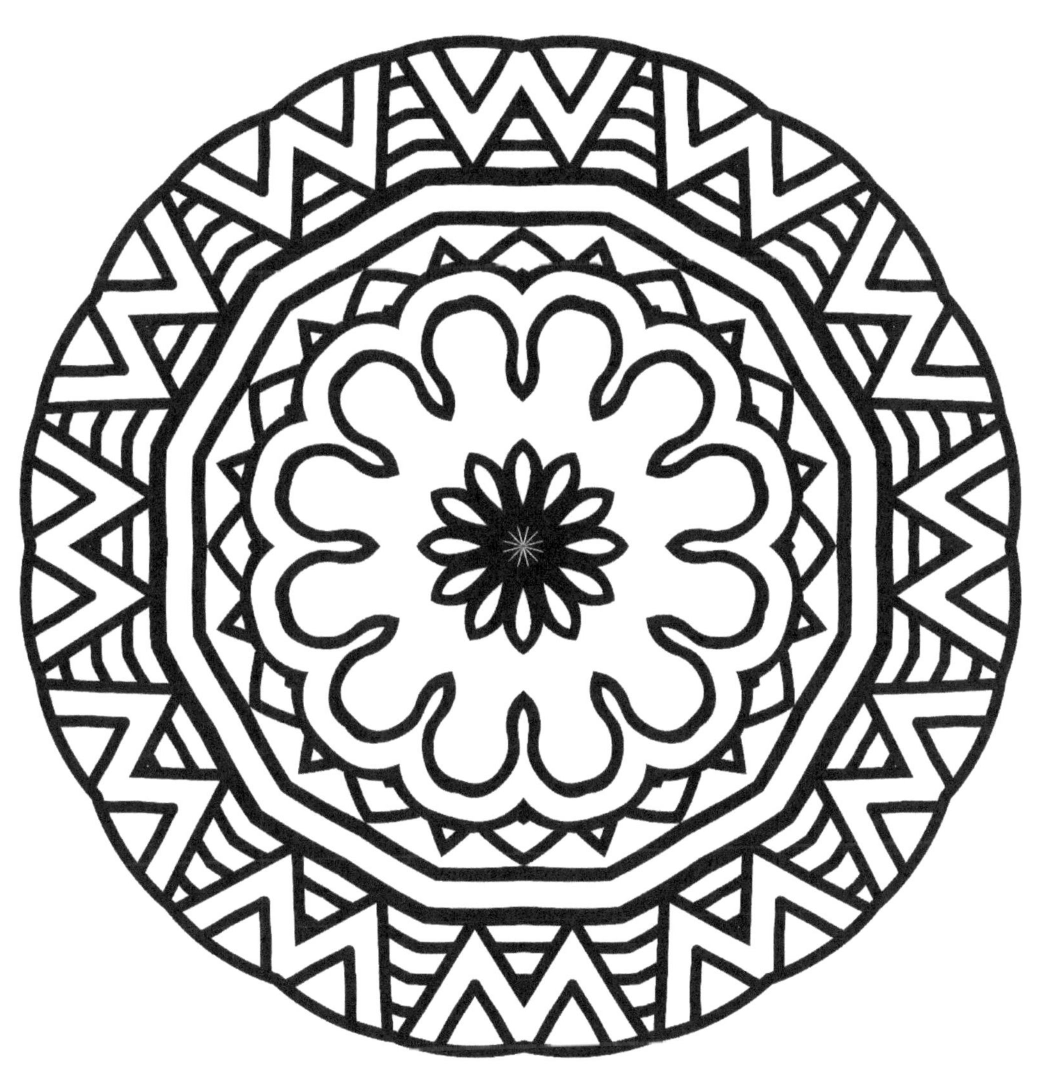

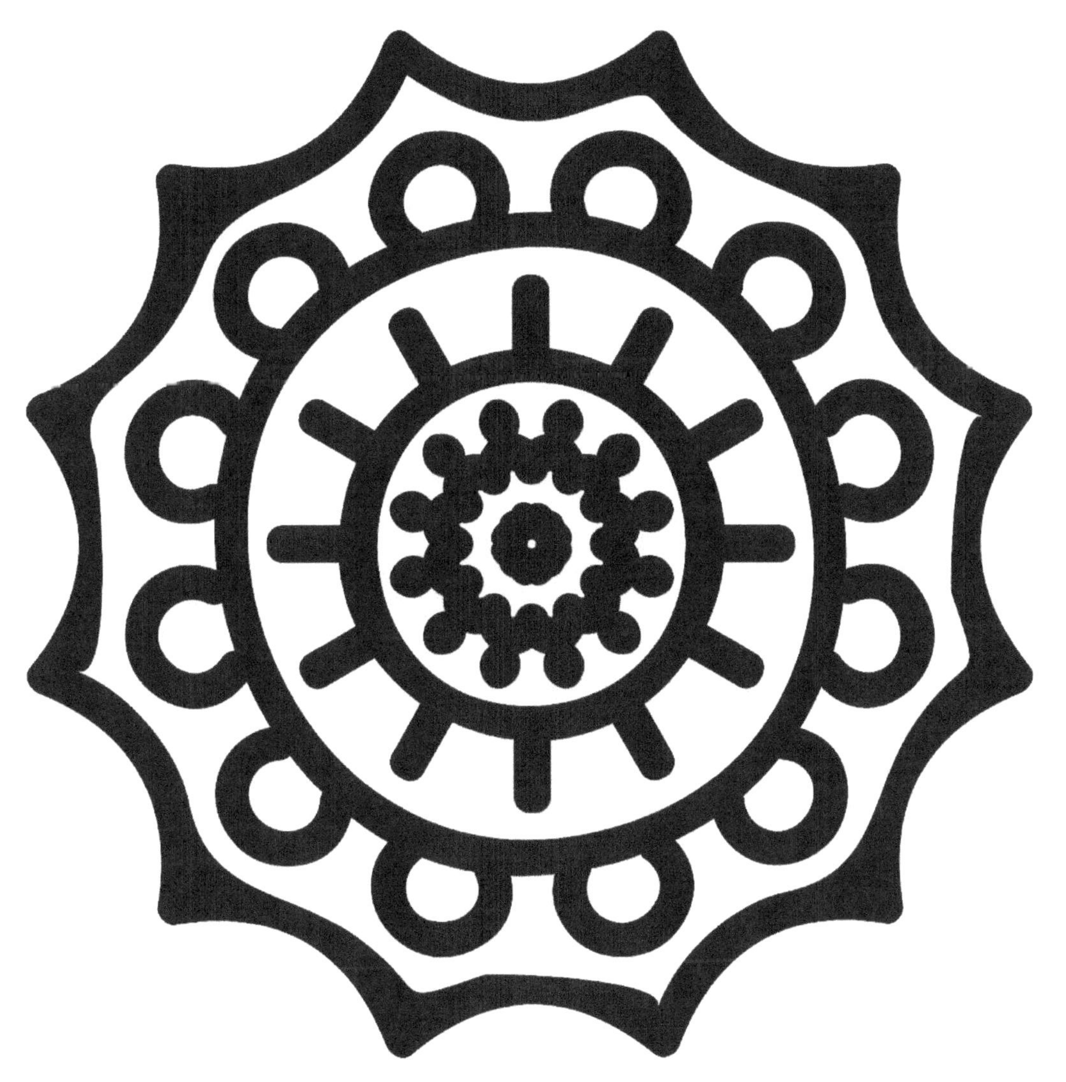

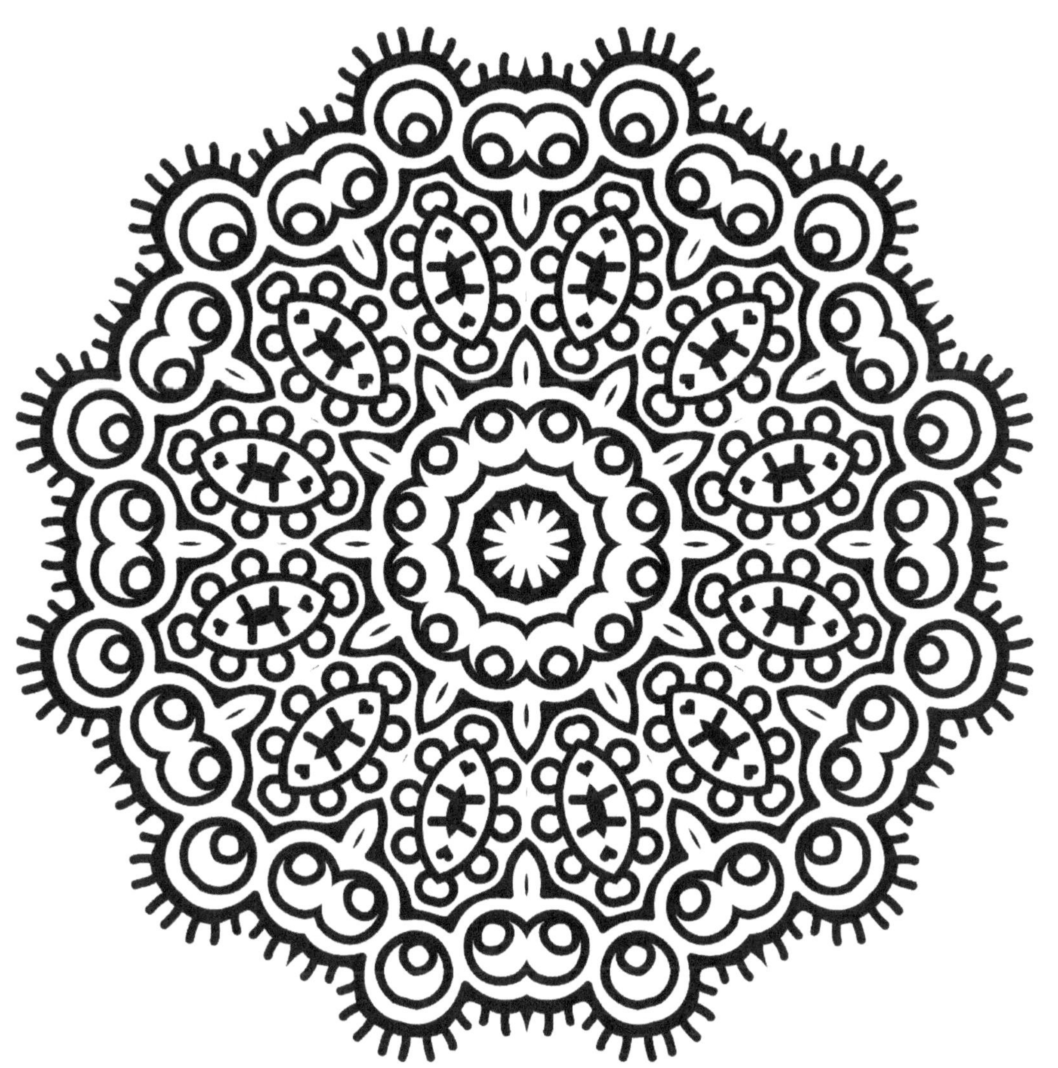

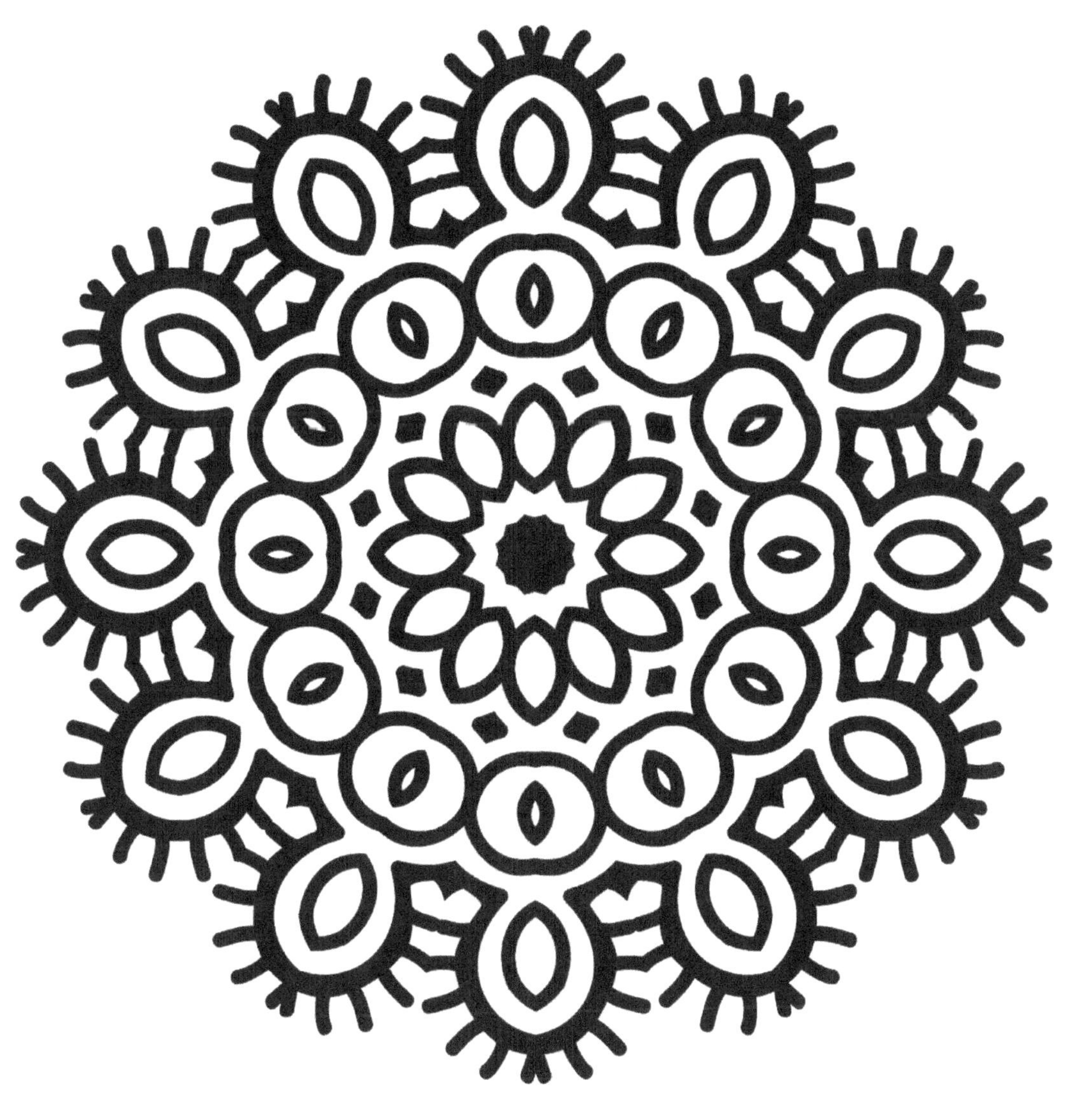

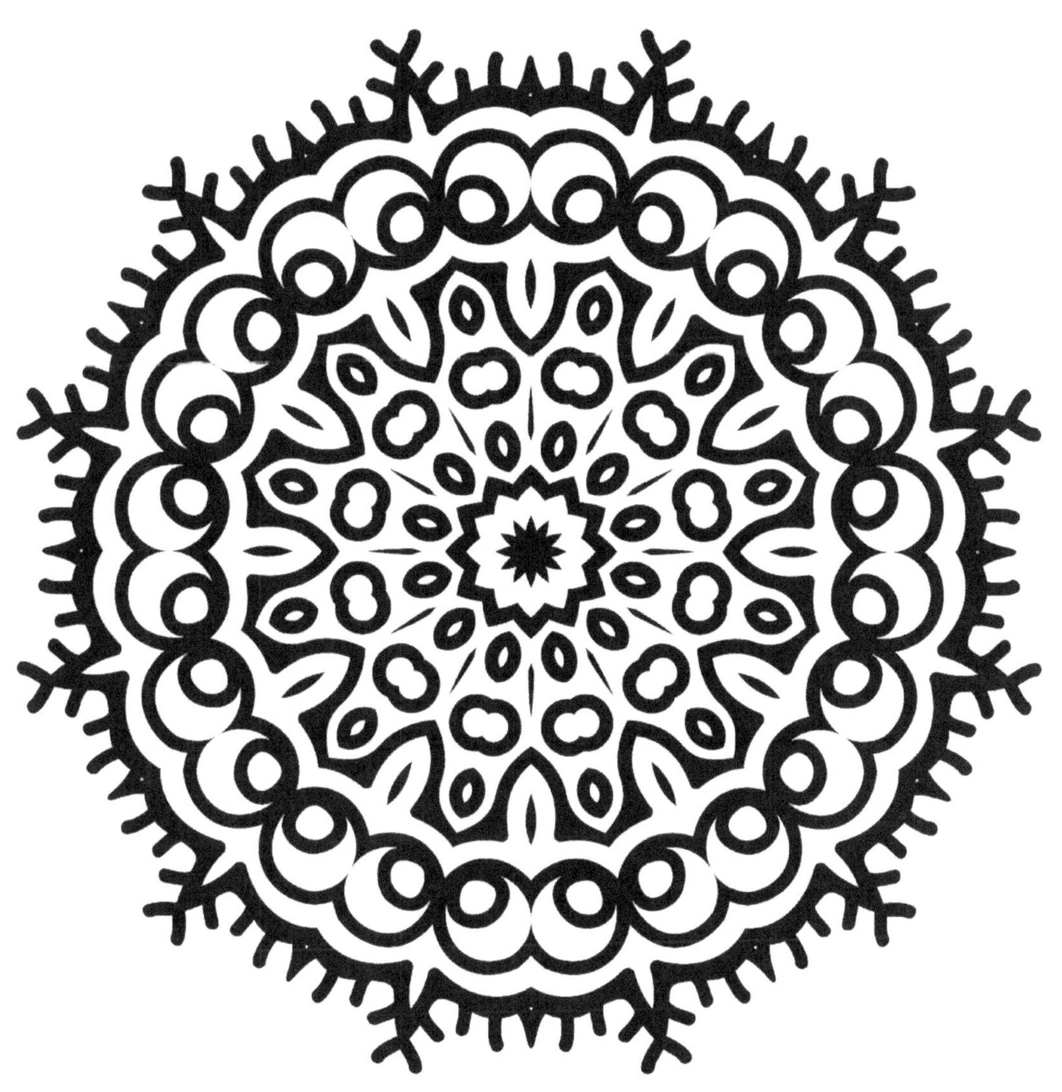

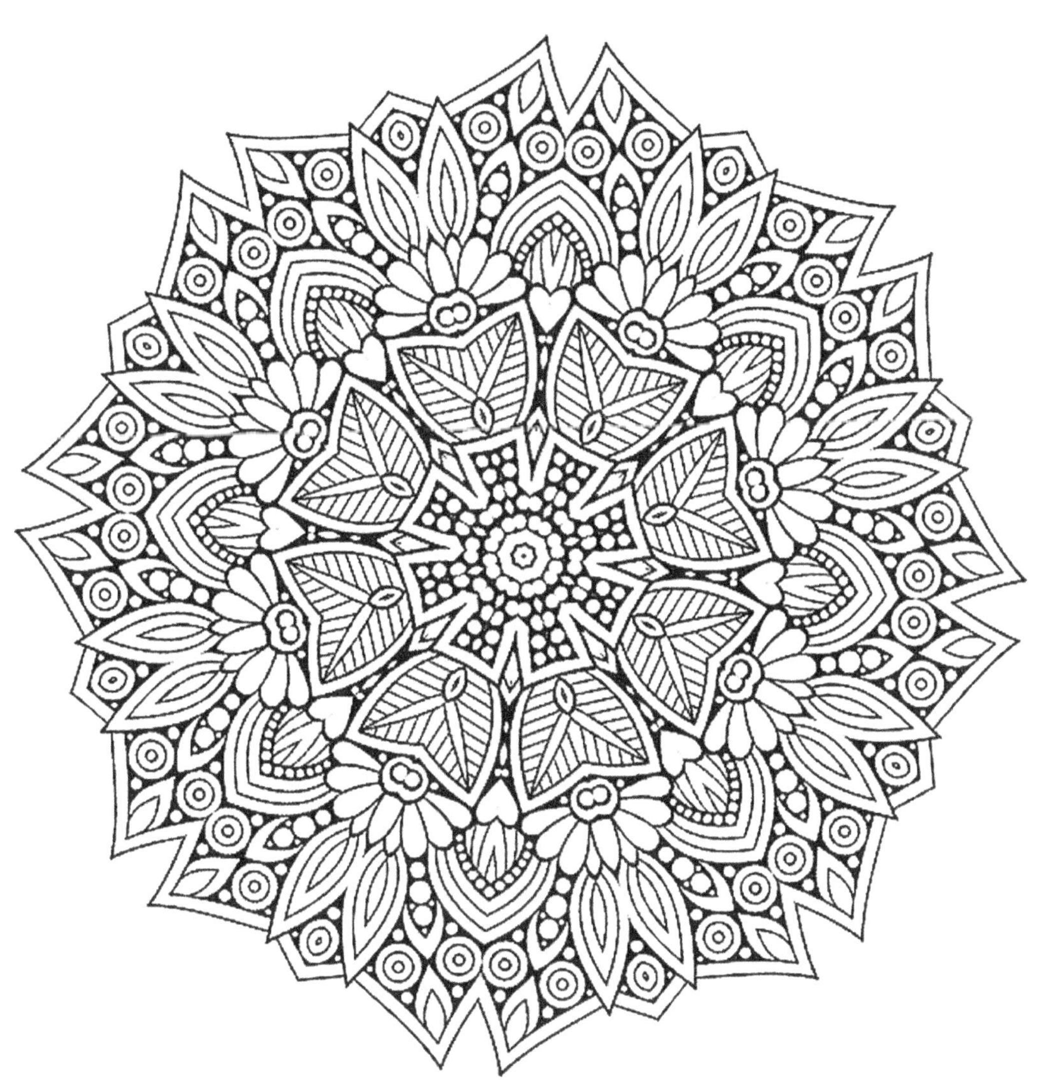

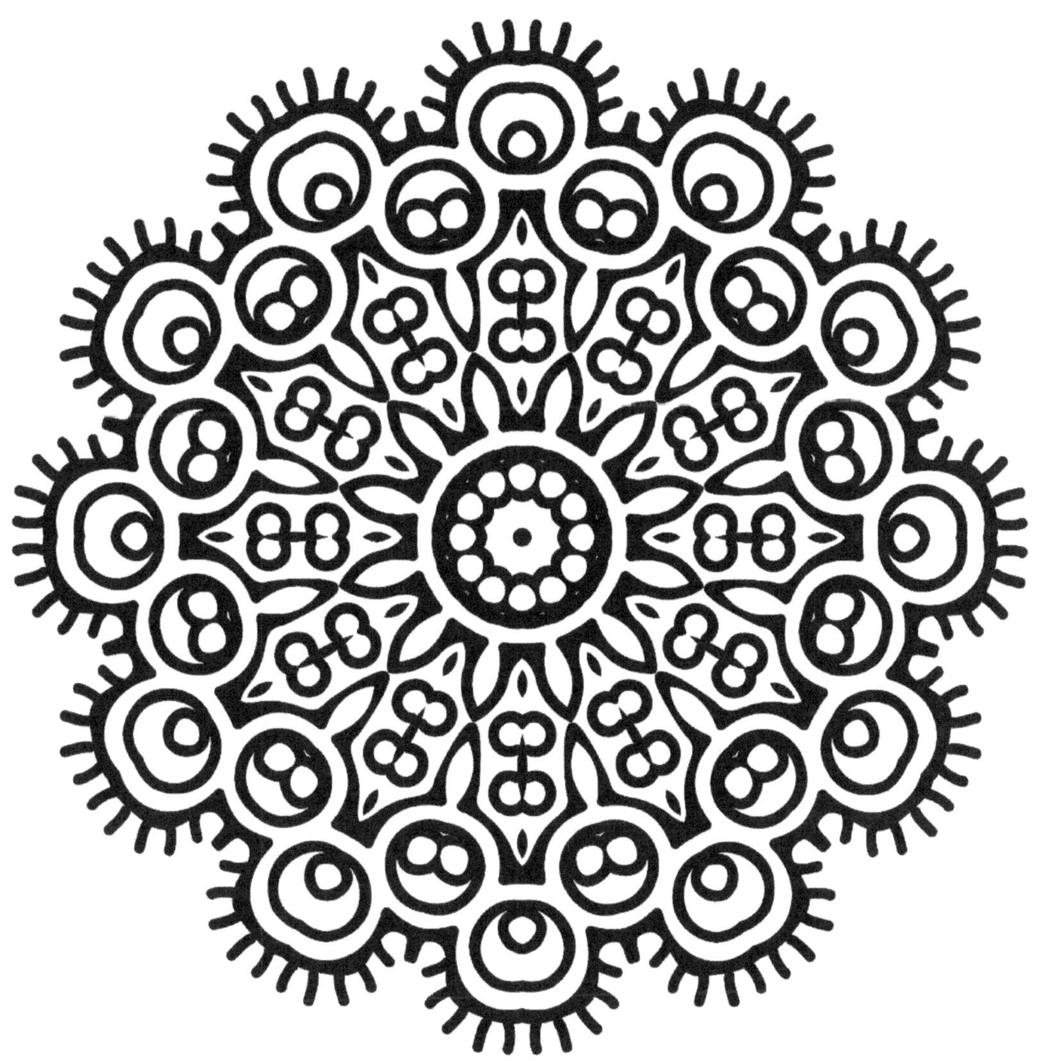

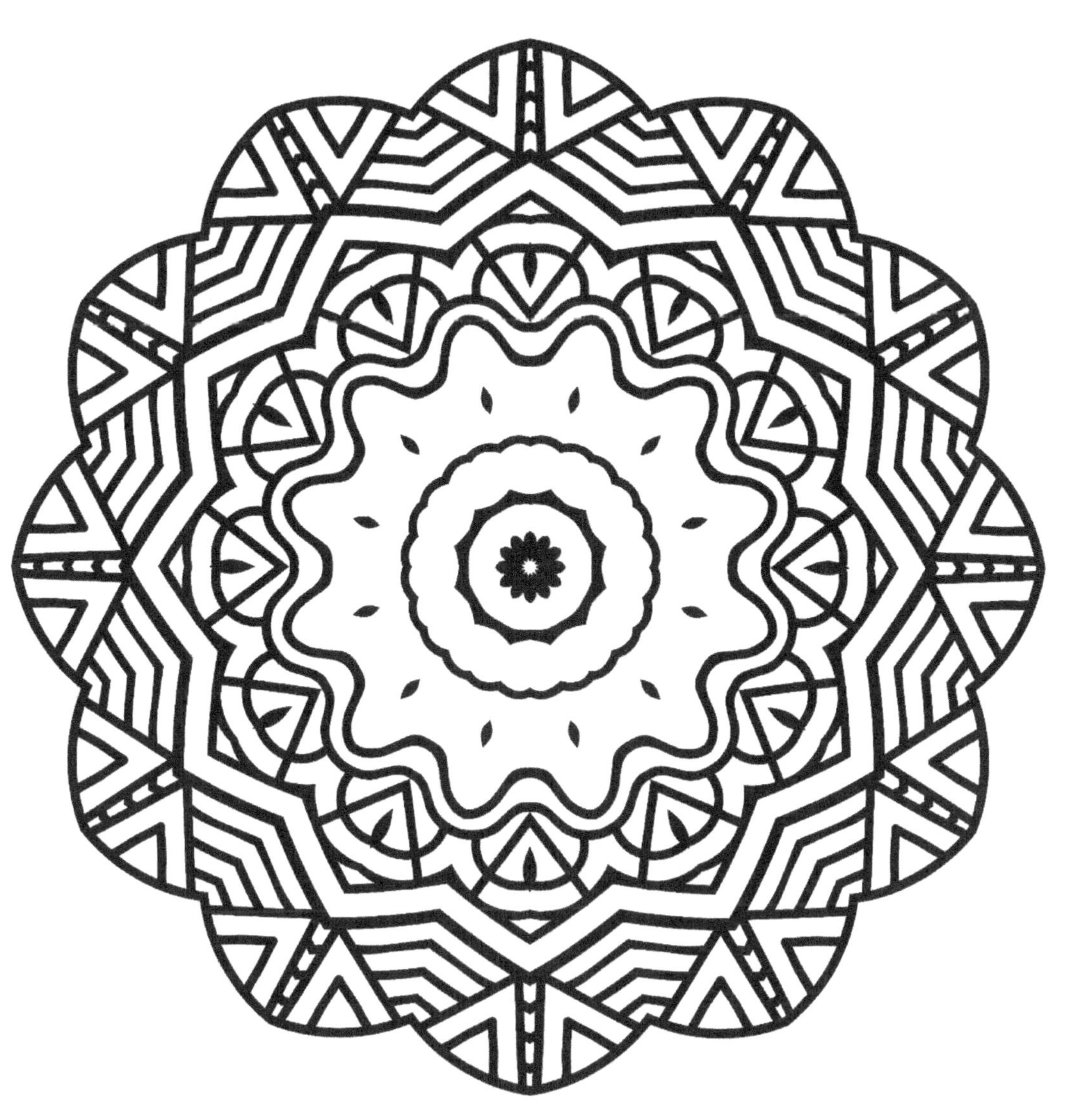

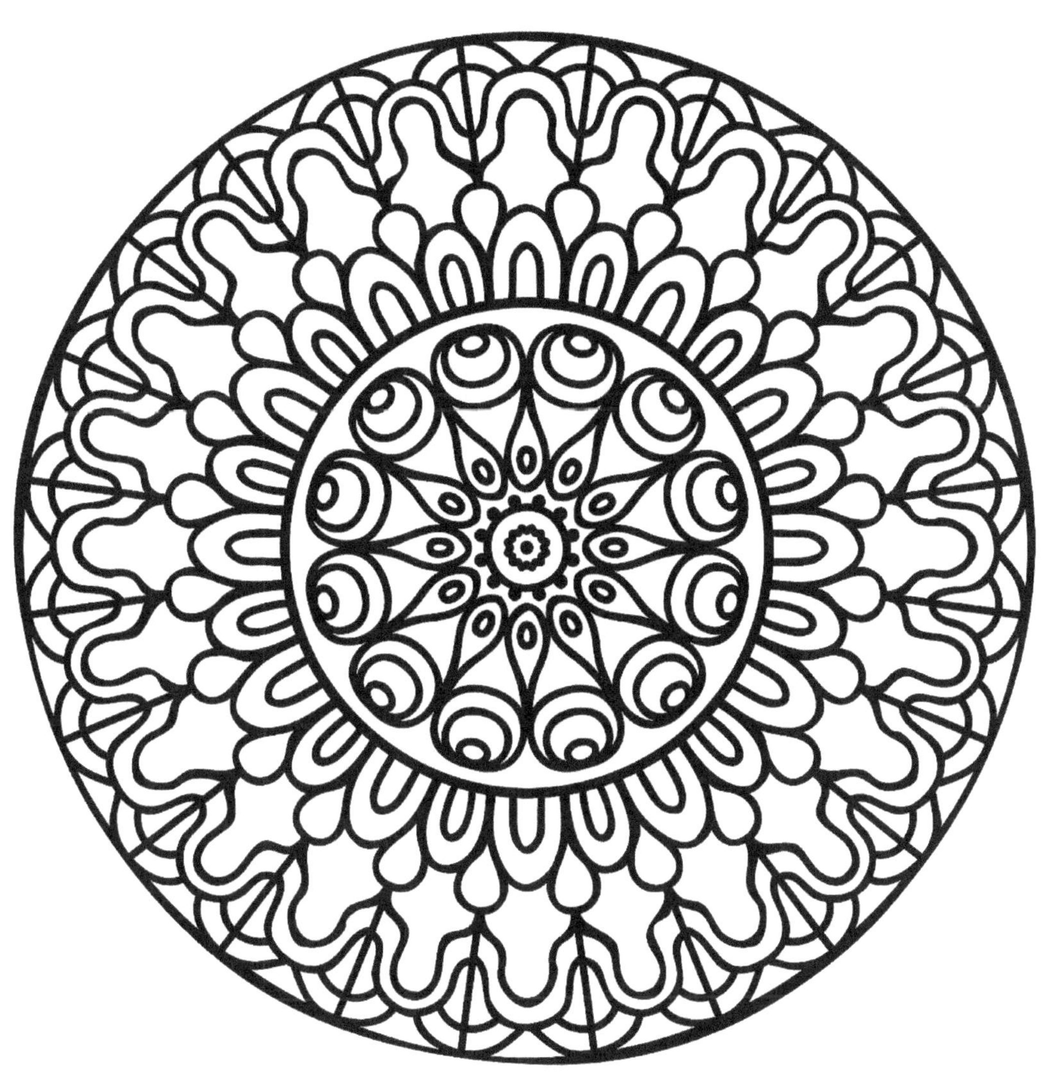

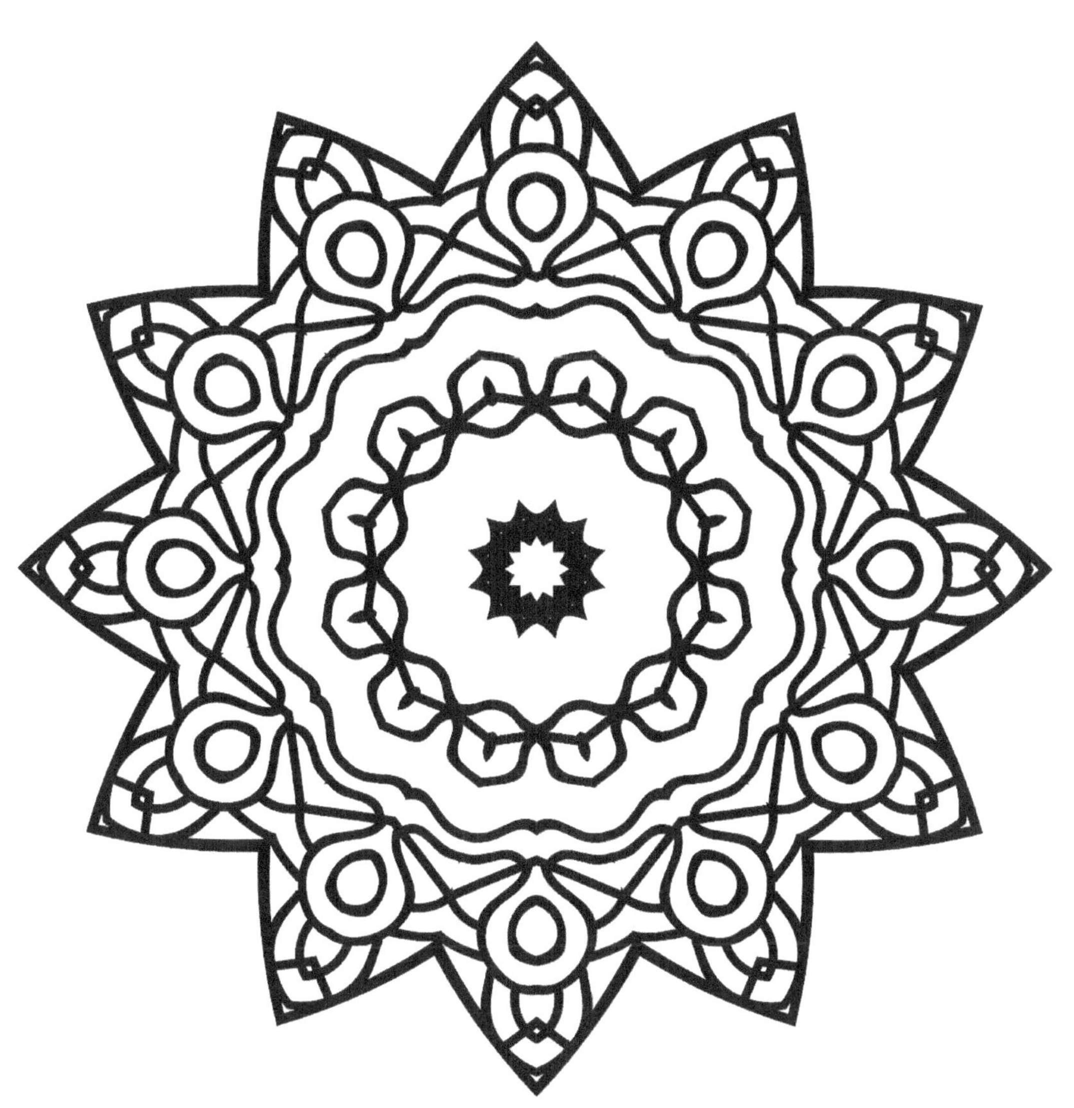

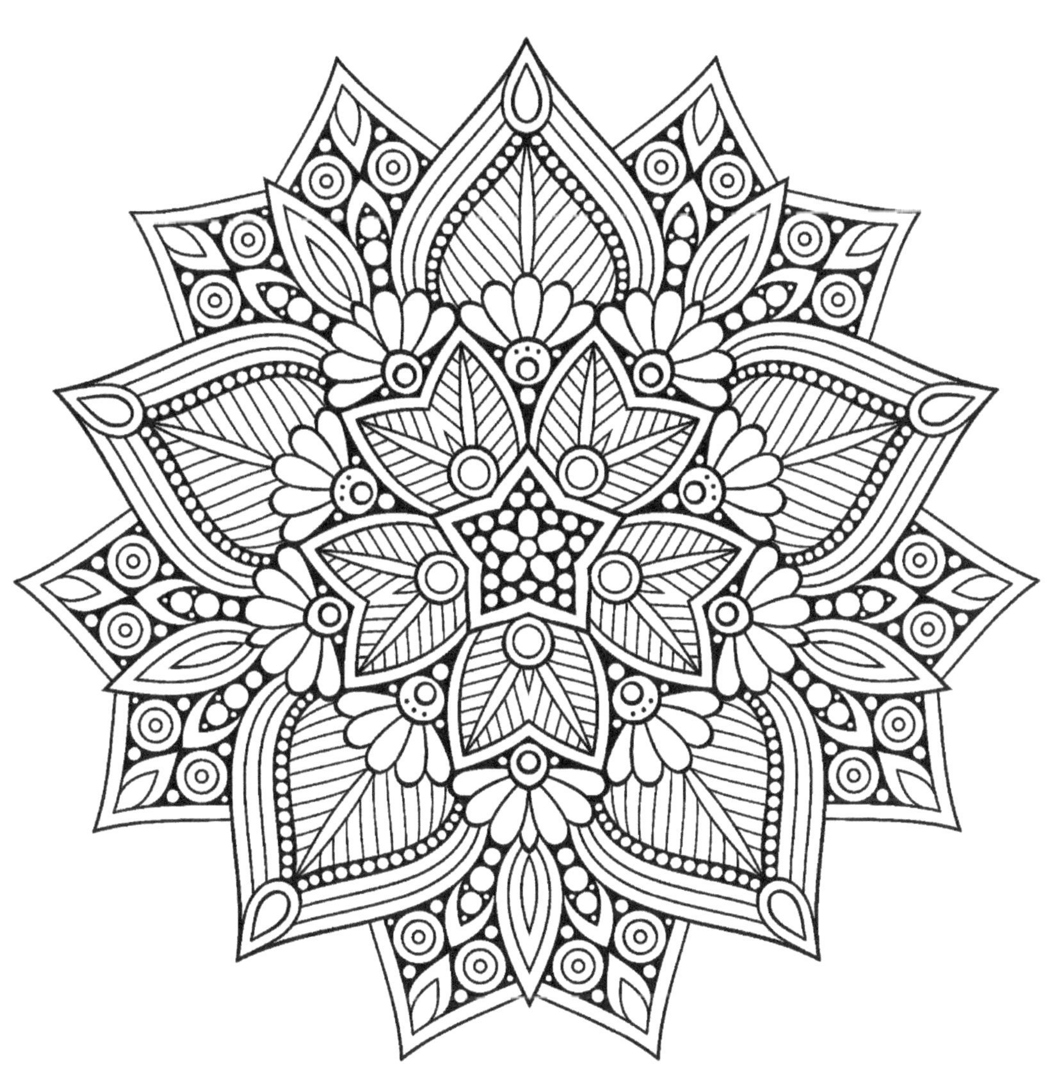

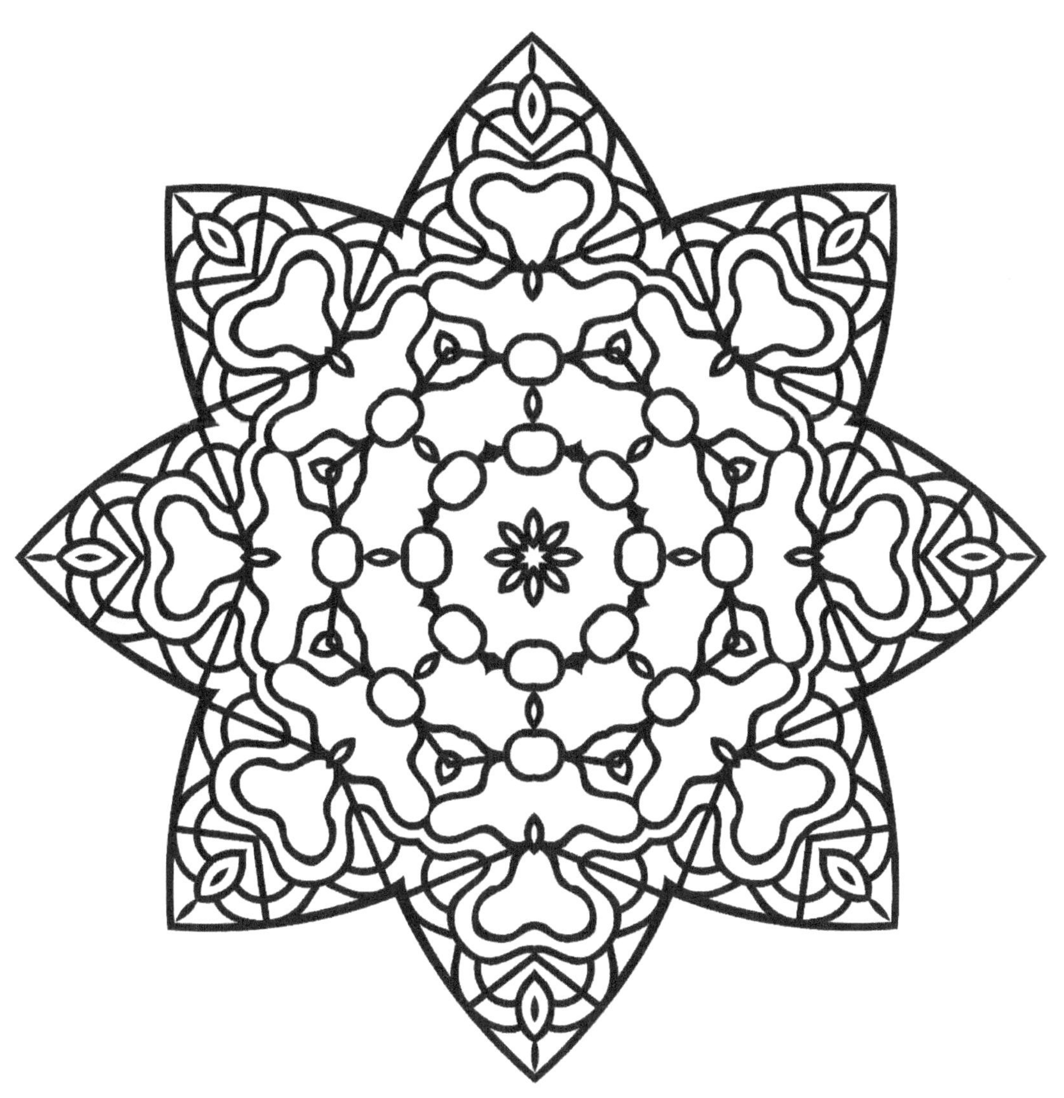

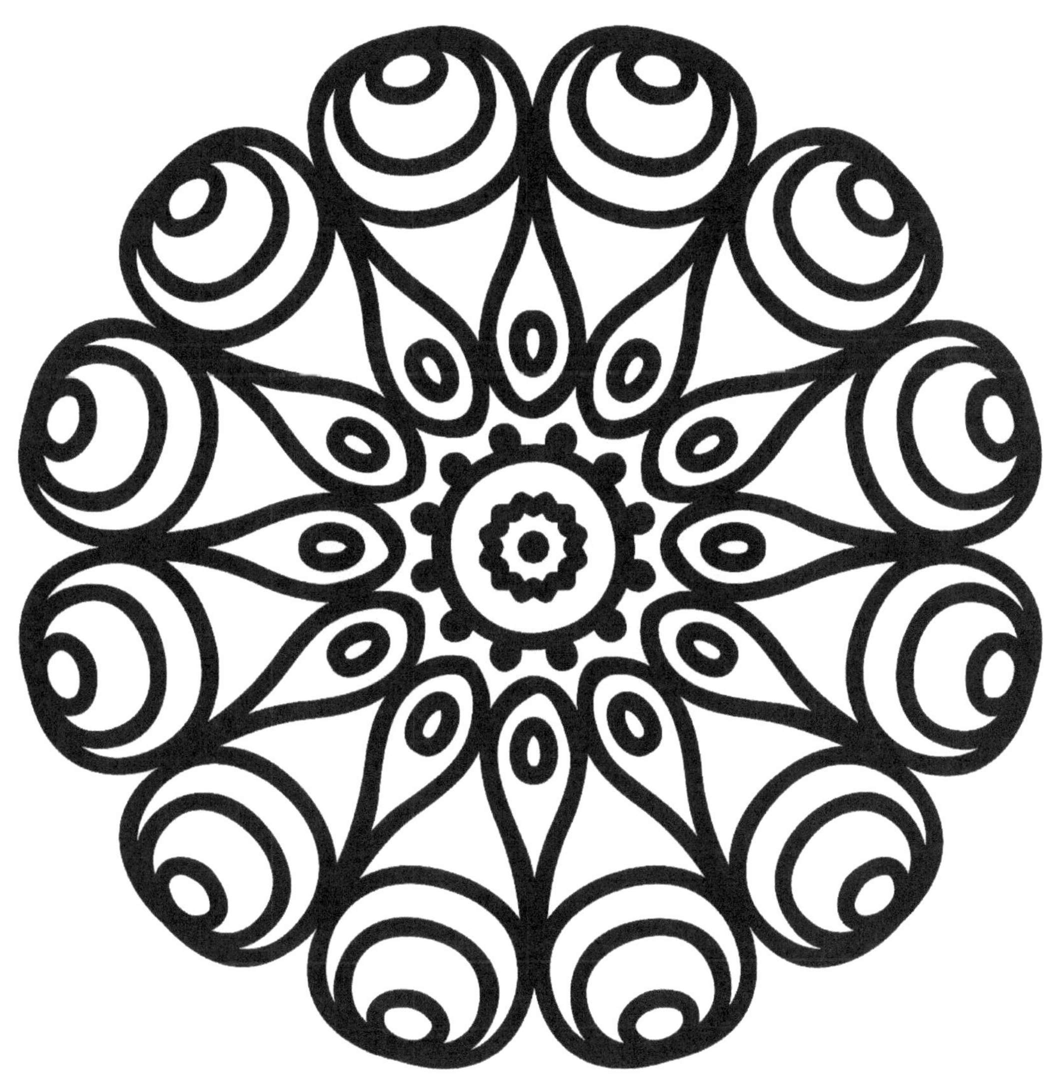

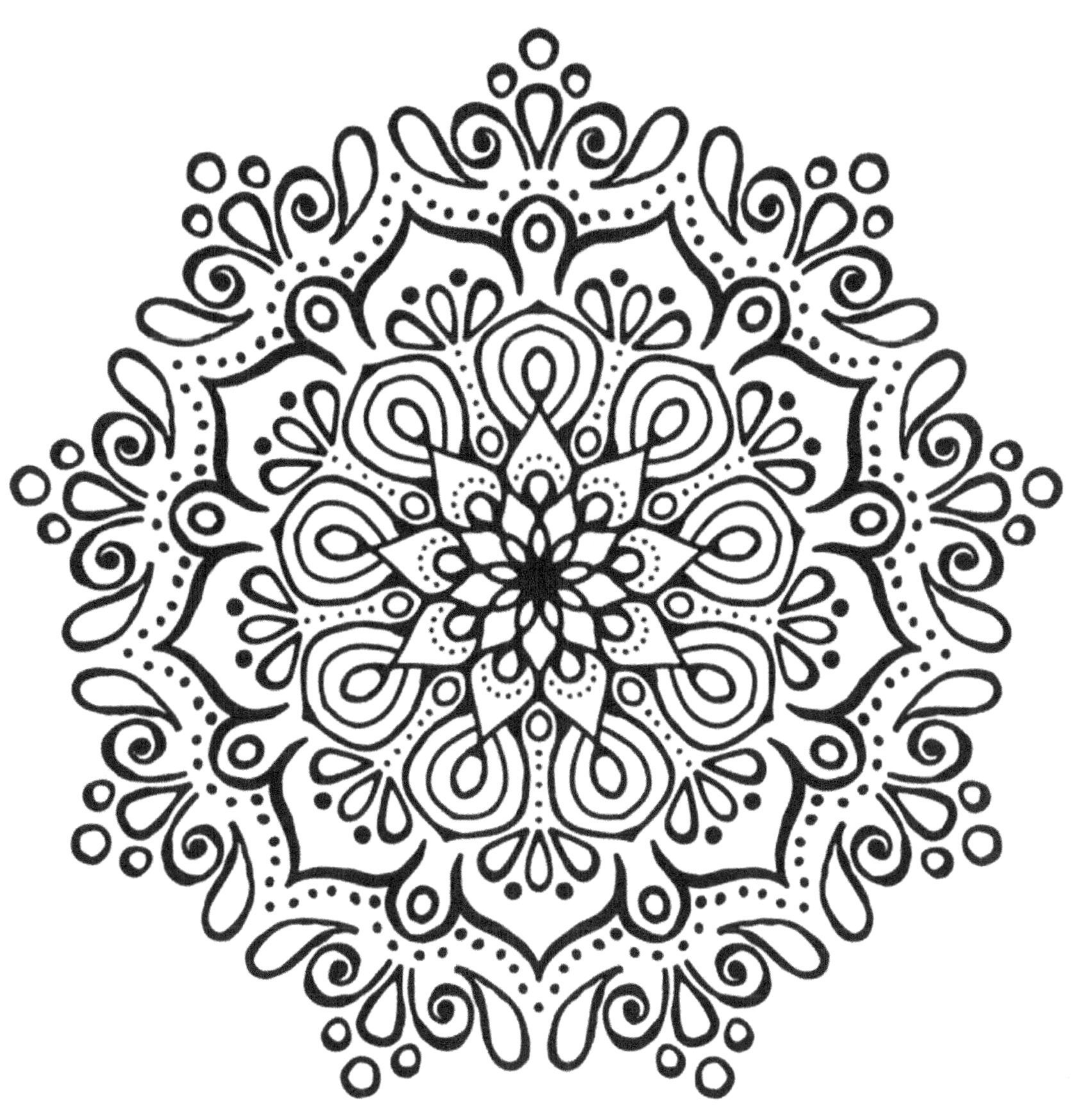

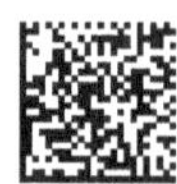
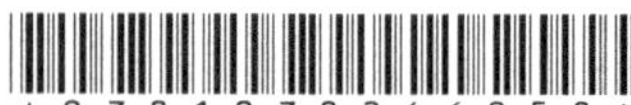